Finding Mr. Right
D.Nile Rivers

Unless otherwise noted, Scripture quotations are from the King James version of the Bible. This book contains material not subject to Pouring the Oil Publications editorial review. The author is responsible for editing, accuracy and content.

Published in New York by Pouring the Oil Publications
P.O. Box 944
Brewster, NY 10509
www.pouringtheoilpublications.com
(203) 300-5152

Finding Mr. Right
© 2007 by D.Nile Rivers

All rights reserved. Written permission must be secured from author/publisher to use or reproduce any part of this book, except for brief quotations in critical reviews or articles.

ISBN: 978-0-9760734-7-5
Library of Congress Control # 2007902827

Printed in the United States of America by Morris Publishing
3212 East Highway 30 / Kearney Nebraska 68847 / 800-650-7888

Dedication

*Father God, thank you for sparing my
life long enough to write these words.
Thank you for keeping me in the midst
of my mess.*

I love you with all my heart.

Table of Contents

Dedication
Poem
Preface
Introduction

1. My First Love	1
2. On My Own	7
3. A New World	10
4. Becoming a Woman	17
5. Motherhood	22
6. A Woman Scorned	30
7. The Real World	33
8. Lust at First Sight	37
9. It's On	44
10. Life Goes On	49
11. Caught Up	54
12. Blast from the Past	61
13. Next Best Thing	66
14. Change of Plans	75
15. Test of Faith	82
16. The Aftermath	101
17. "Divine" Intervention	108
18. Mistaken Identity	113
19. Doing My Thing	122
20. Tunnel Vision	127
21. Dr. Jeckle & Mr. Hyde	132
22. Wolf in Sheep's Clothing	137
23. Hook, Line, and Sinker	141
24. One with the Enemy	145
25. The Beginning of the End	155
26. Finding Mr. Right	163
Epilogue	169

Preface

I was in the middle of writing what would have been my first book (*Being the Man*), when I felt led to write *Finding Mr. Right*. I didn't know anything about writing a book. My only explanation was that God had a divine purpose for wanting me to share. I immediately stopped what I was working on and started writing out the headings for each chapter of my new assignment.

When I started writing, I didn't realize that God would use this experience as a tool to heal unresolved hurts, purge hidden issues of unforgiveness, deliver me from childhood strong-holds, and uncover the hurt from the offenses I had suffered throughout my life. I thought I was just writing about my life in order to help someone by encouraging them with my story. I had no idea. Regardless of what I thought, God had other plans. In Jeremiah 29:11 the Lord says, "For I know the plans I have for you. They are plans for good and not for disaster, to give you a future and a hope." God did more than I could ever have imagined.

Writing this book has done more for me than any counseling session I've ever had. It has enabled me to open up myself to God, and in doing so, He exposed things in me that needed to be removed. He allowed me to see and understand areas of my life that needed to be changed. In other words, He needed to do a work in me so that I could be used for His glory!

It wasn't always easy. I was going through life thinking that I had been cleansed of past hurts, offenses, anger issues, etc., when I wasn't. The more I wrote about the different experiences I went through, the more I realized that I had more skeletons in my closet than I thought.

Yes, I am saved and have repented of my sins (known and unknown), but I'm not perfect. I also understood that when I got saved, there would be a transformation process: changed from being who I was, to who God created me to be. 2 Corinthians 5:17 says, "Therefore if any man be in Christ, he is a new creature: old things are passed away; behold, all things are become new." But the transformation process hasn't ended for me.

Each chapter revealed something I had to learn, and each lesson brought me one step closer to feeling like a whole person instead of broken pieces of a jigsaw puzzle. I never saw myself as broken, until I was able to see God putting the pieces of my life in order. I wasn't aware that I had not grieved over the loss of my second husband until I got to that chapter of my life and had to stop writing because I couldn't stop crying. I was surprised to learn that after four years, I still wasn't over his death. I had to pray and ask God to heal the hurt and anger that I had never dealt with; anger, I had disguised as hurt feelings, as a result of feeling offended over the way he died. I thought I had gotten over his death by telling myself that God took him at a time when he was right with Him, but, subconsciously, I was angry. It took three attempts before I could read through the entire manuscript without having to put it down.

Aside from unresolved issues, the devil tried to distract me with things he had tried in the past, i.e. sex, depression, and health issues. His attempts almost worked, but, because I had surrendered to God's will, he wasn't able to do much. God gave me the ability to recognize the distractions before they were able to overtake me. My initial response was to give in to my flesh (my old tendencies) and do what I normally did, but I was tired of getting the same results. I was tired of going around in circles and finding myself where I started; tired of allowing the devil to use me like a puppet; tired of taking his bait and, as a result, finding myself beaten and bruised from fighting battles that weren't mine. 2 Chronicles 20:15 says, "…for the battle is not yours, but God's." He even tried to mess with my mind. I had moments when I couldn't remember how to punctuate a sentence; I second-guessed things that I knew; I couldn't remember things. He even tried messing with my health which he knew would drain my energy and would cause me to be depressed. As much as I wanted to give in and do nothing, I had to push my way through; I had to praise God even when I didn't feel like it. I had to worship when my mind refused to remain focused on God.

Every time the devil attacked me, I had to fight. I literally had to say, "Devil, get off my back!" Every time I felt like throwing in the towel, or like giving in to the lies, I thought of how I almost died and was able to gain strength from knowing that God spared my life for a reason. I refused to believe that He kept me alive only to have me die after all I'd been through. It didn't make sense, so I called the devil a liar and kept on pushing forward.

By the time I got to the end of the book, God had delivered me from many issues (there are still some left), and had revealed His purpose for my life. But when I thought I was finished and was ready to go to print, something just didn't feel right. In the midst of editing and making plans to go forward, God changed the ending. Thank God I didn't push the issue like I wanted to do (another lesson I'd learned – patience), because it really wasn't about me. Ultimately, I was writing this book because I was led to, because God wanted to use me to reach

His people –YOU: the hurting, the lonely, the hopeless, the needy, the offended, the lost….

Introduction

As a child, I knew exactly who I was going to marry when I grew up. I knew that his name would start with the letter "M" and that we would have children and live happily ever after. Then I grew up, woke up to reality, and discovered all the "wonderful" lessons life had to teach me. I realized that as a child I thought as a child, but as an adult I had to put away childish thoughts. I had to curtail my fantasies so that they were more realistic and appropriate to the present.

As I grew, my outlook on life grew as well. I learned to adapt and overcome situations that life threw my way. I didn't always agree with life; sometimes I got ahead of myself, and instead of focusing on life, I did my own thing, with expectations that life would eventually see things my way. But it wasn't so. Whenever I got ahead of myself, the consequences were always hard to swallow. Imagine someone who thinks she knows everything, except she is the *only* one who sees what she sees; everyone else around her sees the whole picture in an entirely different way. That was me, *Success*. I was convinced about what I knew, and no one could tell me otherwise.

I went through life thinking that I had it altogether. I didn't have to answer to anybody unless I wanted to. I had a major issue with people in authority; I didn't like people constantly telling me what to do. I didn't see the need. Regardless of my dislike, I had to control myself on a daily basis in order to maintain a job. It was the responsible thing to do.

I didn't actively set out to find my "Mr. Right." I was simply living my life. I realize that there are women who actively seek out their Mr. Right. They actually set goals and time frames for when they want to get married, what their mate should look like, what kind of job he should have, the type of car he should drive, etc. I had these same desires, but the older I got and the more experienced I became, I realized that my thinking had placed limitations on what God had intended for me. I realized that my thinking was shallow and superficial.

My expectations limited my focus to the physical qualities of a man. If he looked good, I would entertain a conversation with him. If the conversation was without depth, then I would cast him aside. This way of thinking got me exactly what I sought—superficial relationships based on physical attraction. In other words, I did "seek" and I did "find" exactly what I was looking for—heartache and disappointment.

I got saved when I was fourteen, but I didn't really understand what it meant. The preacher said that if I confessed with my mouth that Jesus Christ was Lord, and believed in my heart that He was raised from the dead, that I would be saved. Saved from what? Saved from going to hell. I didn't want to go to hell, and though I wasn't quite certain there was a hell, I wasn't taking any chances.

Going to church wasn't a choice. Mom made me go whether I wanted to or not. When I left home and was old enough to make my own decisions, I didn't step foot in a church building. I rebelled and did things that I wasn't allowed to do living at home with Mom. I didn't think about God until I was about twenty-two years old and in desperate need of help. Like many people do, I turned to God because I needed Him to get me out of a bind, never mind the fact that I hadn't acknowledged Him since I was a teenager. And when He got me out of the bind, I didn't need Him any more. I went right back to doing what I normally did.

I wanted to do right by God, but I had a major issue with sex. When I slipped, I repented, but I repeatedly found myself at the altar for the same things. I thought, "If I can't be good all the time, then I'll just be bad all the time." I didn't want to be a hypocrite. Sound familiar?

It's been seventeen years since I first tried living as a Christian. I finally got it right. Praise God, He never gave up on me. For He said in Hebrews 13: 5, "...I will never leave thee, nor forsake thee." It took a while, but it finally began to make sense and I was able to accept God's purpose for my life (rededicated my life to Jesus Christ in 2000). It has been one heck of a journey. The devil hasn't stopped trying to win me back to his side. He's tripped me up a few times, I've made decisions because I was deceived, I made numerous mistakes, had sex without being married, drank, and partied, but I refused to go back to being the person I used to be. Every time I fell, I repented, learned from my mistake and dealt with the consequences. I kept on going.

Here I am, thirty-nine years old, married three times and widowed once. Will I ever get it right? Whatever happened to the happily ever after: the house with the white picket fence, the two and a half kids, and the family dog?

Chapter One

My First Love

Mom made us (my siblings and I) go to church whenever she had the chance. We went, but we didn't pay attention. Most of the time we, the teenagers, sat in the back of the church passing notes, reading romance novels that were stuffed in between the Bible pages, or walking back and forth to the bathroom. We seldom understood what the preacher was saying. The only time we listened was when we were forced to go up for prayer and when we felt compelled to be saved because we didn't want to go to hell. We repeated the sinner's prayer when we were told. Doing so meant we would be saved, but we really didn't understand what it meant to be saved. By the time we left church, we usually didn't even remember we had repented of our sins. We were teenagers.

After a while, I didn't mind going to church, especially after the first time I realized that boys were more than something to make fun of. Up until the age of fourteen, boys were nothing special to me. I hung out with them because I liked to do many of the same things they liked: climb trees, ride bikes, climb buildings, fish, play soccer, and build things. I liked to compete with them to prove that I could do anything they could do, if not better.

It wasn't until I went to church one night and saw a boy that caught my eye, that my feelings towards the opposite sex changed. I didn't let on that I liked him. I was still getting used to the whole idea of boys being more than competition. Finally I had my reason for going to church. I didn't tell Mom, but she noticed my change in attitude. She didn't say anything.

Little by little I let him know that I liked him. Whenever I saw him in church, I made it my business to seek him out. His name was Cecil,

D.Nile Rivers

and he was a sight to behold. He looked like a bodybuilder. He had big legs, a wide back, huge arms, etc. Let's just say that he was nicely proportioned everywhere! His hard work and dedication to his body was evident and he knew it. I wasn't the only girl interested in Cecil. It didn't matter to me at the time. I didn't know the first thing about liking boys, so I fell back on my tomboy ways in order to get close to him. It worked. We had similar interests which meant we had things we could talk about, unlike the girlie girls who were too busy trying to look cute to get next to him, but couldn't.

The only time I saw Cecil or got to talk to him was when I went to church. Whenever there was a church function or outing, I volunteered to go.

Things changed when I started going to high school and became friends with Cecil's sister, Adrienne. I didn't know she was his sister until I went to visit her one day and ran into him. Well, lucky me! Could it be that it was divine intervention? Nope, more like opportunity for temptation.

I was always over Cecil's house visiting, so it was only a matter of time before I fell in love with him. I guess it was destined to happen even though I didn't know the first thing about being involved with a boy. Instead, I did whatever I could to be around him. If it meant sparring with him during his karate practices or lifting weights, I was there.

Cecil liked me, but I wasn't sure to what extent. Two years had passed since we met and I was ready for more than playing games. I still didn't know any more about relationships than when I first met him, but it wasn't about that any more; I was tired of the teasing.

On my seventeenth birthday, I went over to Cecil's house. I had made up in my mind that I was ready to do something about the constant teasing and agreed to meet him in the basement. I was nervous. I didn't know anything about having sex, except the stories I had heard from other girls who said that it was painful at first, but it eventually got better. I didn't know if it would be anything like what I had experienced when I was molested as a child.

After much hesitation and shyness on my part, Cecil finally calmed me down and reassured me that he would be gentle, and he would stop any time I wanted him to. When he got on top of me, I stiffened as I anticipated and prepared for the pain. I was just as afraid of having him on top of me as I was when I was a child, but this time it was consensual. He was so large that I was sure there was no way he was going to get that thing inside of me. But he did, and it did hurt, just like they said it would. He didn't take long, though, and I was glad when he was finished. I pulled up my pants, got on my bike, and rode home as fast as my little legs could pedal. I couldn't bear sitting on the hard bicycle seat, so I rode standing up the entire fifteen minutes home. When I got in the house, I went straight for the bathroom to clean up and saw the evidence that alerted me to the fact that I had indeed been a virgin. I thought the escapades of my childhood had deflowered me, but they hadn't. I cleaned up and hoped that no one would notice the difference in me. I just knew that it would be obvious. I had read so many romance novels, and had learned that women usually had a glow about them after having sex. I kept checking the mirror to make sure I wasn't glowing because I didn't want anyone to know.

The next day I told his cousin, Linda, and she was shocked to learn that I had waited so long to have sex. Apparently, I was a late bloomer, but fear of getting pregnant and what Mom would do to me if I did, held me back until that day. Well, I wish I had continued to be afraid because after that one time, I was hooked! Sex was like a drug, and I couldn't get enough. Whenever we could find a spot or the time, it was on. I was feigning for him like an addict.

My infatuation with Cecil didn't last long. Once he started going to my high school it was all over. He was out of control. He came to school dressed in sleeveless shirts to show off his biceps. This stunt drove the girls crazy. I had already gotten used to him so it didn't bother me, but the attention changed Cecil. The attention I had been giving him was nothing in comparison to an entire school full of teenage girls. It didn't take long before I realized that I couldn't compete and simply backed myself out of his life.

I was still infatuated with Cecil, but things weren't the same. He became arrogant after all the attention he received from the girls at school. I saw him whenever I visited his sister, but things were strictly plutonic between us by this time. He was no longer interested with my teenage crush on him. This became painfully apparent when he tried to hook me up with one of his friends. One night, while I was visiting, he lured me down to the basement where his friend was waiting in the dark to have sex with me. Once I realized what their intentions were, I got out of there as quickly as I could. I had a few choice words for him the next time I saw him. I couldn't believe he would do that to me. It

D.Nile Rivers

showed me just how much he really cared about me. I was nothing more than a notch on his belt. This brought an abrupt end to my infatuation with Cecil. But because he was my first, I knew there would always be a special place in my heart for him.

After graduating high school, I joined the Army and lost touch with Cecil. When I returned three years later, I decided to look him up. We made an attempt to get together, but it just wasn't the same. It wasn't special any more and I came to realize that our time had long passed.

We lost touch and my only knowledge of him was through his mother and his sister with whom I had remained friends with over the years. They told me that he had gotten married and had moved down south.

Ten years later, when I asked Cecil's mother about him, she told me that Cecil had gotten saved, and was speaking and preaching the Gospel. I was shocked, but also very happy for him, because, I too had finally realized what it meant to saved, and was living as a Christian. To think of the many days we spent in church because our mothers made us go. How we complained for having to be there for what seemed like hours every time "the church doors were open." It finally paid off! Well, the Bible does say in Proverbs 22:6, "Train up a child in the way he should go: and when he is old, he will not depart from it." Our mothers knew what they were doing, even if we didn't agree with it.

Unfortunately, Cecil was in jail as a consequence of his former lifestyle. When he got saved, he decided to return home and turn himself in to settle any outstanding offenses he had against him. Though it was the right thing to do, it wasn't necessarily something he was looking forward to, especially since he was now married and trying to raise a family. But God was in control, and he knew that God would keep him.

I decided to visit him one day. I asked his mother to mention to him that I wanted to see him and to ask whether it would be acceptable for me to do so. His sister told me that none of the family had gone to see him and that his wife rarely got to visit him as well because she still lived down south.

My first contact with him was through a phone call. He called and left me a message on my voice mail. I didn't recognize the voice at first, but after replaying the message, I realized it was him. I was so

Finding Mr. Right

excited. I felt like a teenager all over again. I was disappointed that I hadn't gotten to speak to him, but he had indicated that he would try again. Try he did and it was so good to talk to him after having been out of touch for so many years. We made arrangements on the phone regarding my visit, and I told him that I looked forward to seeing him the following weekend.

I was a little nervous going to see him. I had forgotten what he looked like and was a little concerned about how our visit would go, but I was determined to see him and to let him know that I still cared and didn't mind spending a few hours to visit him.

I didn't know how long we would have during the visit. I was counting on a couple of hours, so I wanted to make sure that I got there at the beginning of visiting hours, one o'clock. I got there on time, but I wasn't aware of the procedures or the rules and, apparently, I didn't have on the right attire (I had on a shirt with a logo on it.). But the guard had pity on me because I had never been there before, and I was allowed to go in after waiting for an hour or so. Once I got into the visiting room, I ended up having to wait another half an hour before he finally arrived.

I tried not to keep looking at the door while I waited for him. I wanted to see if he would recognize me first. The door had been opening and closing for other prisoners for the entire half hour I had been sitting there, but *this* time, when it opened, I knew it was him. I slowly turned around and saw him walking towards me. Wow! He was a sight to see. He was even bigger than I remembered, and he had a lot more hair than I had ever seen him with. I wasn't sure if I was allowed to touch him so I sat there until he stood in front of me and asked, "Aren't you going to give me a hug?" I stood up nervously and gave him a brief hug.

When we sat down, we simply looked at each other and smiled. We had to sit with his right knee touching the outside of my right knee. I was a little uncomfortable. I don't really know why I felt that way, but I did. I apologized for the delay in getting through the guards, but he told me that visiting hours ended at six o'clock. Well, when I heard that, I decided that I would stay as long as he liked.

We talked until we got caught up on each other's lives, and as we talked I couldn't help but smile because he was not the same boy I knew back when. He was a grown man now. He still looked like the Cecil I once knew, but he was a totally different person. When he

D.Nile Rivers

spoke, he captivated me. His knowledge of the Bible was amazing. His memory was even more amazing. He quoted Scriptures as if they were just normal conversation topics, and when I didn't understand he explained what he meant. It was refreshing and pleasing to be in the presence of this new Cecil.

I stayed and we talked and shared while he ate. The best part of receiving visitors was the opportunity to eat the food provided in the visiting room. I came prepared. His mother had informed me that I should bring money so that he could eat.

After visiting for a few hours, Cecil told me that he had to go because he had to use the bathroom, and it just couldn't wait any longer. I didn't see the problem. He explained that once he left the room, he would be subjected to a full body search prior to returning, and he wasn't in the mood to go through it. We decided to call it a day. But before we went our separate ways, we prayed together, and it was a moment I will never forget. The Spirit of God was truly with us as we prayed. As he prayed for me, I prayed for him that God would continue to strengthen him and keep him while he continued to serve out his time.

I left promising to visit again and to write. I didn't get the chance to see him again. I tried to go back, but his mother told me that he wasn't receiving visitors. I wrote a few times and he responded, but that didn't last either. His mother told me that he was released the following year.

Fin∂ing Mr. Ri*g*ht

Chapter Two

On My Own

May 1985, the last month of my senior year in high school, I had no idea what I wanted to do with my life. I was seventeen years old and I didn't have a career picked out. No career meant I wouldn't be going to college. I decided to join the Army instead. I told Mom that I wanted to join the Army, and I met with a recruiter. Once I passed my entrance exam and decided what I would do in the Army, Mom signed the papers, and after graduation, I was on my way.

Basic training was in South Carolina. I was excited because I hadn't traveled out of Massachusetts since I arrived in 1981 from the Bahamas. I didn't know it, but Basic Training would be an experience that would change my life.

I had no previous knowledge of what to expect, but I learned, soon enough, that I would have to change my way of thinking and doing things. For the most part, things were different, but not hard. I had to become disciplined, which meant I had to march to their drum and their tune and not my own. The basic things weren't hard. I was given orders to follow, and I did. I was given rules to follow, and I did. I was shown how to do things the way they were expected to be done, and I did. But there were things I didn't agree with, and I wasn't afraid to express how I felt about them. Of course, this was not acceptable, and there were consequences, but it was all part of growing and learning discipline in the environment I was in.

For example, I just couldn't understand why I had to be punished for someone else's mistakes. I couldn't understand why they had to wake us up so bloody early in the morning. I couldn't understand why we had to do the same exercises over and over again *and* every day! Then one day it clicked. I wasn't an individual any more, but part of a

7

team. I belonged to a platoon that consisted of all females, and we did everything as a platoon. So if someone screwed up, we all paid the price for that one individual. I learned that it was up to each individual in the platoon to watch out for the other and to make sure that we were on one accord at all times in order to be successful as a platoon.

I had a lot to learn, but I was willing. I was determined to "be all that I could be." So, whatever we had to do, I did to the best of my ability. Whatever the challenge was that came my way, I was always gung ho and tried to appear fearless on the outside. I succeeded at it, too. I was so outgoing that my peers nicknamed me "GI Jane."

I was determined to pass Basic Training and move on to the Advanced Individual Training (AIT). I was told that AIT would be mostly classroom work, and I would actually get to train with the guys instead of only women. Of course, I didn't think I would be able to catch the eye of any guy the way I looked during training. I had to wear a hat every day, which meant that my hair was always a mess. I also had to wear Army issued glasses. They were called rape protector glasses or RPGs because they were so ugly. In other words, you were guaranteed to be safe and single.

My RPGs didn't make much of a difference, somehow I attracted a guy while I was in line waiting to call home one day. We corresponded for a little while, but it never went anywhere. That was fine with me because I wasn't really interested.

The only time we were allowed to be around the male soldiers was during mass services and when we had down time to use the phone to call home. I called home often to speak to my family and to call my boyfriend, Blackie, whom I had met two months prior to leaving for Basic Training. Blackie was four years my senior. We met while I was working at Burger King my senior year in high school. I called him Blackie because he was extremely dark, but he was very handsome. What attracted me to him was his sense of humor. He was always imitating Eddie Murphy and making me laugh.

Blackie was also in the Army, but he was a reservist and only had to go one weekend every month for drill. I fell in love with him quickly, but before I knew it, I had to leave for training. I called him whenever I could, and wrote him every day.

AIT began directly after Basic Training. We didn't get a break to go home or relax. We were told to pack up our things and were marched over to another side of the base where we would live for the

Finding Mr. Right

next two months. Once AIT started, I began to lighten up a bit. I still complained about the meaningless things they had us do: pick cigarette butts off the ground, pick up trash, scrub the showers with toothbrushes, etc., but we also got passes to go to the club and sometimes off the base. We also got to mingle with the guys, which was an additional plus.

One day I called home to speak to Blackie and his father told me that he had moved out and had moved in with his girlfriend. I was devastated. I had only been gone two months and not only did he have someone else, but he had moved in with her. I was hurt, but I quickly bounced back.

Blackie and I had never slept with each other, and I think that was the main reason I was able to get over him as quickly as I did. Finding another love interest also had a lot to do with it. Some how I was able to catch the eye of another male soldier in my unit. I wasn't attracted to him at first. He had bright pink lips and all I could think of was buying a dark shade of lipstick so he could tone down the pink. It sounds vain, but it was how I felt and my feelings prevented me from getting to know him sooner than I did. It wasn't until I looked in the mirror one day and saw how horrible I looked, that I woke up to reality. I looked really bad. I realized that he had to be interested in something other than what I looked like. I immediately forgot about being vain and was able to see past his pink lips. He was attractive, had a deep, Barry White voice, could sing like it was nobody's business, and could dance like Fred Astaire.

I remember exactly when I fell in love with him. One night, while we were at the club, Heatwave's "Always and Forever" was playing, and as we slow-danced, Cooley sang along to the song in my ear. Wow! He was even better than the group singing the song! His singing and his slow dancing did it for me. From then on, we were an item. Even though the guys and girls weren't supposed to mingle like that, we couldn't stop our emotions.

When AIT was over, and it was time to leave for our various destinations, I was heartbroken. I just knew we would never see each other again, and I couldn't bear it.

Cooley went home to Florida and would be going to Colorado for his assignment. I went home to Massachusetts prior to being shipped out to Germany for my assignment.

We stayed in touch while we were on leave for the Christmas

D.Nile Rivers

holidays. Cooley even sent me a sweatshirt marked "Cooley's Girl" on the back. I was so proud.

Finding Mr. Right

Chapter Three

A New World

When I got to Germany, four months later, it was a totally different atmosphere than what I was accustomed to. I was in a different country and very far from home. I was also on my own for the first time in my life which meant I would be making my own decisions and Mom wouldn't be around to stop me. It was a scary feeling. Even in Basic Training I had someone telling me what to do. Now, it was up to me.

I was unleashed into a new world with very little experience about life. I quickly got used to being in the Army and to working a full-time job. It was a job like any other, except the training wasn't the average training, and we had ridiculous schedules and duties that were sometimes unreasonable.

I got into the swing of my new life and with that came a lot of men. I wasn't used to having men approach me like these did. I mean, some of these guys were so gorgeous that I couldn't believe they were actually trying to talk to me! I wouldn't say that I had a self-esteem problem; they simply had so many women to choose from. I got used to them and the attention, but I wasn't experienced with men like the other girls. I wasn't aware of their tricks or games. I wasn't aware of their lies either.

I didn't mind having fun though. I went out with my friends on a weekly basis. We went to the clubs whenever we could, and I tried a different drink every time I went. I even tried smoking while in the club to make it seem like I was older than my mere eighteen years. I flirted with the guys and danced the nights away whenever possible. The Army didn't seem to care what we did, as long as we reported for duty (were in formation) sober and on time.

The German culture was something new to me. I didn't like the

11

D.Nile Rivers

food, but I enjoyed visiting their castles and country sides. I didn't care for the aggressiveness of the people when I went shopping, but I learned to adapt by walking with both of my hands on my hips with my elbows sticking straight out at my sides to allow me all the room I needed when I walked among them.

Aside from going to the clubs and coming home in the wee hours of the morning, we played touch football, went to the movies, played drinking games, bought music and played it at high volumes out our barracks room windows. There was only one English-speaking channel on the television, so a lot of people were having sex at night instead of being entertained by the tube. This meant that a lot of the girls were getting pregnant.

When Cooley finally came to Germany, a year after I arrived, I couldn't wait to see him. He wasn't stationed close by, but I didn't mind driving out to see him. We tried to hook up at clubs, but other than that, the only time I saw him was when I made an effort to see him.

When he finally came to see me, nothing happened. Instead, he left me and went to visit this guy I had introduced him to one night while we were out. Cooley asked why he was the only guy hanging out with so many women, and I told him that he was gay. Funny thing, he had been hanging out with us for a long time, and it never dawned on me that he was gay until someone told me. I was a little confused at first because he was married. I couldn't understand why he would have a wife if he was gay. I was still so naïve, but I caught on as time went by. His wife was gay, too.

The following morning some friends told me that they had seen Cooley walking off the base with this same guy. I was momentarily confused, but it didn't last for long. I never mentioned to Cooley what I knew and I never asked him about it. Let's just say that after that day, my hopes for a relationship with Cooley changed.

I didn't lose too much sleep over this change in our relationship. There were just too many men to choose from and what seemed to be so little time.

I spent the majority of my life hanging around with girls and not having a boyfriend in high school because I was never pretty enough or I was always too skinny. Well, once I got to Germany I started going to the gym and lifting weights. I joined the track team, and ate all the hamburgers I could stomach to help me gain weight. I got contact

Finding Mr. Right

lenses so I wouldn't have to wear glasses, but they were the hard contacts and they constantly popped out of my eyes whenever they wanted to, so I didn't wear them much. Instead, I walked around blind. I couldn't see who any one was from far away, but I learned to recognize people by the way they walked and their build. Later I learned that guys thought I was conceited because I would pass them by or I wouldn't respond to them if they waved at me. I had to confess to them that it wasn't that I was being conceited, but that I just couldn't see far away.

As I put on weight, I filled out in all the right places. I even started taking birth control pills (also contributed to my weight), which I didn't know anything about until my friend mentioned them to me. I wasn't having sex because I didn't have a man, but with the way things were looking, it wouldn't be long.

It was a given that if you went to the club you could find a man and even go home with one. I was picky. I knew what I liked and what I didn't like. I went to the clubs to dance. I loved to dance. I hadn't been allowed to go out when I was growing up, and I loved music and dancing. So when I got the chance to dance or listen to music, that's exactly what I did. If I met a man in the club while I was doing both, and if they were interesting or cute, then I would talk to them. I didn't really trust men that much at this point, so I wasn't very eager to be involved with another one any time soon. I didn't mind looking and admiring them though.

One night, while I was in the club, I met this absolutely gorgeous man. He was light-skinned with a nice body, nice hair, pretty teeth, pretty eyes, etc. I couldn't believe he was actually interested in me. But he was. I danced with him a few times and would have given him the time of day, but when it was time to leave, he got into a fight with a drunken man who kept bothering me. I was visibly upset by what he did and when I asked him why he had done it, he said, "Well, that's what they do in the movies to get the girl." I couldn't believe what he said. I knew his actions weren't because he cared about me. He didn't even know me. He did it to impress me and I wasn't impressed. He walked me back to my barracks and when we arrived, I dismissed him. He wasn't pleased at all. He actually thought he was going to have sex with me as a reward for what he did. Didn't happen!

Aside from going to the clubs all the time, the next best thing to do was go to the post team basketball games. The guys were a sight to see,

D.Nile Rivers

and it was entertainment at its fullest.

During that first year in Germany, the team was so good that they made it to the championships. As fans, my friends and I followed the team wherever they went. I had an ulterior motive for going. There was a player on the team that caught my eye. He was about six feet and two inches tall, light-skinned, with a low, wavy hair cut, chiseled face, and a body that uttered poetry with every movement. Let's just say that in appearance, he was pure perfection. God pulled out all the stops on this specimen! I was so taken by him that I was determined to meet him. So one night after one of the games, I asked my girlfriend Fran, if she would speak to him for me and let him know that I was interested in him. She was more than happy to oblige me. I watched her walk over to where he was and engage him in conversation. I don't know what they talked about, but when she came back she told me that he wasn't interested. I shrugged it off until later on that night, when I saw him coming out of her room. I couldn't believe it. I was hurt. I wasn't used to people being so conniving. I had a lot to learn, and learn I did.

I didn't let Fran know that I had seen him coming out of her room. I never let on that I knew how low and dirty she was. I just tucked the information away and became more aware.

Life went on as usual on the base. We continued to party, drink, work, meet new and interesting people, and I continued to learn the ropes of life. I learned that, to some men, women were nothing more than a piece of meat. On this base, we were considered "fresh" meat because we were the latest batch of women to arrive. So for the time being, we were ripe for the picking. We constantly had guys interested in us and we had a lot to choose from. I actually had the opportunity to be picky. It was great!

One night we went to the club like we normally did. While I was sitting at the table with my best friend, Nique, who I had met in Basic Training, and Fran, guess who walked in? Yes, the basketball player that I had asked Fran to speak to on my behalf. He walked with just enough arrogance and dressed with class to match. He put the "oo" in cool. He was all that, a bag of chips, and a drink. He was the whole Happy Meal! I didn't say anything to Fran. I simply watched him as he walked towards the back of the club to the bar.

In the meantime, the three of us sat at our table, chair dancing and waiting for men to approach us to dance. At this point in my life, I was

14

Finding Mr. Right

still in the learning phase and hadn't gotten to the point where I was bold enough to dance by myself. That would come later. If my girls and I weren't dancing together, then I was dancing with some guy who had asked me to dance or someone I knew from my unit.

As we sat there, we had men ask us to dance and we picked and chose which ones we wanted to dance with based on how they looked and whether or not we thought they could dance. Sometimes we said "No," and other times we said "Yes."

I kept hoping that the basketball player would come over and ask me to dance. I hadn't seen him dance all night, but I was hoping that maybe he would dance with me. I sat there trying to look as grown up as I could with a drink in my hand. Every so often I would accept an invitation to dance, but I was constantly looking around to see where he was. When I finally had enough of waiting, I made my way to the back of the club to get a drink and to accidentally bump into him. As I got nearer to the bar, I saw him near the left corner of the room with a drink in his hand. He wasn't talking to anyone, just standing there enjoying the music. When I finished getting my drink, I made my way towards him without actually making it seem as if I was approaching him. I came up from behind him and stood on his left side.

I said, "Hello." He responded in kind. I said, "I was wondering if you might want to dance later?"

He said, "Sure."

Of course I wanted to leap and touch the ceiling, but I kept it cool. I didn't want him to know that I practically worshiped the ground he walked on or the very air that he breathed. I pointed out to him where I was sitting and told him that whenever he heard a song he might want to dance to that I would be there waiting for him. He said, "Okay," and I left.

I walked away from there trying not to run as fast as I could. I literally had to will my legs to move at a normal pace. When I finally made it back to the table, I was cool. I didn't say anything to either of my friends. I especially didn't want Fran to know that I had spoken to him.

The waiting was difficult, but I did what I could to remain calm and tried not to keep looking towards the back of the club. I didn't want him to think that I was anxious, even though I was having trouble staying in my seat. Men came by and asked me to dance, but I turned them down. I had my eye on one man only, and that was it!

D.Nile Rivers

When he finally came and asked me to dance, I continued to act like it wasn't a big deal. Fran's mouth dropped open, and I simply ignored her and followed him to the dance floor.

As we danced, I tried to keep it cool. I think he knew, either from seeing me dance previously or just from observation, that I was trying to be a little conservative with my dancing. He said, "Don't make me look bad." I smiled and tried to pace myself and my moves with his so it didn't seem like I was trying to out dance him. It was truly a chore for me to act cool when I felt like a pressure cooker about to explode from shear excitement over the fact that I was actually dancing with him. He had no idea how long I had wanted to meet him. How could he? It's not like Fran told him anything!

We made little conversation as we danced. He asked me my name, and I asked him his. His name was Reece. I told him that I had seen him during the basketball games and that I had asked my girlfriend to speak to him on my behalf some time ago. He looked confused. I looked over towards the table where Fran was sitting and I explained to him that I had asked her to give him a message one night after a game. He said, "I never got the message." He said, "I remember your girlfriend, but she never mentioned anything about you." I took this all in and tucked it away in my mind with the other information I had gathered on Fran.

The song was almost over, and I kept hoping that he would want to dance to another and another and another. I never wanted the song to end. It wasn't so much because of the conversation we were trying to have, but simply because I had waited so long to meet him, and I still couldn't believe we were actually dancing together. When the song ended he danced with me for another song and as we danced we just smiled and silently flirted with each other. It was great, and I loved every minute of it because I knew Fran was watching and more than likely wondering what we were talking about. But like they say, all good things do come to an end and so did our dance.

When I went back to the table, all eyes were on me. They both knew how much I adored this man and for me to have had the opportunity to dance with him was the ultimate experience at that point in my life. They wanted to know what we talked about, but I didn't have much to say. My mind was way beyond the dance. I was busy trying to figure out how I was going to see him again.

For the rest of the night, that was my mission. To figure out how I

Finding Mr. Right

was going to continue what I had started during the dance. It wasn't time to be shy or naïve; it was time to be an adult or at least a young lady pretending to be worldly and all knowing.

By the time the club was closing, I had somehow managed to be bold enough to seek him out in the crowd. Now you have to remember that I didn't have my glasses on and couldn't see very well from far away. So the people in the club all looked alike to me except for shapes and sizes. That didn't prevent me from finding him again. I approached him and got into a conversation with him. From that conversation I told him what barracks and what unit I was with, and that was the beginning of a whole new life for me.

Chapter Four

Becoming a Woman

From that night on, Reece and I became an item. I was young and inexperienced; he was seven years older than me and had a bit of a head start. Our initial conversations included questions about whether or not I was a virgin (it made a difference because he didn't want me falling in love with him and acting crazy) and the usual questions regarding past boyfriends, family, etc. He didn't mention much about himself. At that point in time, it didn't really matter because I was too smitten to care.

I soon learned that Reece was all about image. I had to look good at all times, which meant I had to dress sharp, wear makeup all the time and have my hair done. One day he came by the barracks to visit me, and I didn't have any makeup on. He made a comment about it, and I simply told him that I was in my room all day and wasn't going anywhere. He quickly put me in check and told me that it didn't matter because I never knew when he would come by. I found this a little strange, but shrugged it off as if it made sense.

Word soon got around that I was Reece's girl. Whenever we were out, he made sure to show me off to his friends as if I was a trophy. Speaking of his friends, they weren't really friends. He pretended that they were, but he didn't trust easily which meant they were more than likely in his life to benefit him in some fashion and not necessarily for their friendship. Reece always seemed to be a few steps ahead and always thinking or planning something. I'm sure his friends didn't notice, but I picked up on it.

Things weren't always great, but it was a learning experience. I was used to being a certain way, and grew up living a sheltered life, so I was easy to deceive. Though I pretended to know things, I was really

Finding Mr. Right

learning as I went along.

Reece molded me into the woman he wanted me to be. He had me so wide open that I would sit on the window sill in my room for hours, looking out to see if his car went by. Or I would wait in my room hoping he would come by and visit. We didn't have cell phones back then, so I couldn't call him at the drop of a dime or whenever the thought crossed my mind. Basically, I waited around the barracks hoping someone would knock on my door to tell me that I had a phone call.

The barracks were set up in such a way that the only available phone was at the front desk and the CQ on duty, the person in charge of quarters, would take messages or send someone to give us messages. If we needed to use a phone, we were expected to use pay phones.

In my barracks, the male soldiers stayed on the first and third floors and the females had the second floor. Males were not allowed on the female floors, and vice versa. Of course this didn't stop anyone. It wasn't unusual to find soldiers of the opposite sex sneaking around on floors and in rooms they had no business being in.

If someone had a visitor of the opposite sex, they simply signed in as if they were going to visit someone of the same sex and detoured to the actual person's room they wanted to see; a simple solution to an inconvenient rule. The only problem was not to get caught. If the CQ went around checking for visitors in the rooms they signed into and the visiting party wasn't there, then you had a problem.

The first time Reece and I had sex, I was hooked. I did the shy thing because being with him was new, and I wasn't very experienced. But he wasn't having that. It was put up or shut up! That's not what he said, but it was understood. I knew that I couldn't play games with him because he could have any woman he wanted the way he looked, and if I was going to be with him I would have to be woman enough to be with him.

Reece took advantage of the fact that I was young and inexperienced. I filled him in on my past so he was aware of my childhood and my past flings. But no one in my past had been like Reece. Everyone prior to him had been my age and too young to play the games he was about to play with me.

Whenever I could see him, I did. We went on drives, I hung out at the movie theater where he worked off base (he took on a civilian job to earn more money), we saw each other at the club, and we went to

19

D.Nile Rivers

hotels when we wanted to be intimate. I had a roommate who was always in my business, so I preferred not to do my business in the room when I knew she would be there.

I'll never forget the first time Reece stayed over. The following morning, while we were still in the bed, my roommate came over from her side of the room (our room was set up with two wall-lockers, side by side, in the middle of the room as a partition to allow privacy) to have a conversation with us. She came over, holding up lingerie panties in her hands, to ask his opinion! I couldn't believe her. She was uncouth and truly had no manners. I say that, not just because of what she did then, but because of who she was and how she carried herself around base. She wasn't a stranger to the men on base. Based on her actions on that particular occasion, I decided not to invite him over again.

After being with Reece for about three months, a friend of mine who knew that I was seeing Reece, asked to speak to me. He asked me if I knew that Reece was married.

I said, "What? He's not married."

My friend looked at me with a serious face and shook his head yes indicating that he was. I told him that he was wrong. I accused him of not knowing what he was talking about. He told me, "His wife is in my unit. She just arrived." He even knew where they lived. I couldn't and didn't want to accept what I was hearing. He told me to ask Reece. I told him that Reece had never told me that he was married. He didn't act as if he was married. He didn't wear a wedding band. As far as I knew, when you're married, you are supposed to wear a ring.

It hadn't occurred to me when Reece moved off base into housing, that the only reason he was allowed to live in housing was because he had a dependent or a spouse. I didn't know because I was naïve and still not up to speed on the military and its regulations or policies. Not only did he have a wife, but I was told that he had a girlfriend in his unit as well. This was killing me. I was so blind.

Well, I couldn't wait to see Reece after work that day. When I confronted him he simply said, "You never asked."

I was baffled. I looked at him as if he had two heads. "I didn't ask?" I said, "Aren't you supposed to act like you're married if you're married?" He knew exactly how naïve I was and counted on it. When I asked him about the girlfriend, he said, "She is a friend who happens to be a girl." Basically, she bought him the expensive things that he liked.

20

Finding Mr. Right

I provided him with sex and paid for the hotels we visited and bought him clothes, and his wife, being married to her allowed him to get more money from the military and got him out of the barracks.

As hurt as I was over the news, and even though I knew better, I couldn't stop seeing him. I was in too deep, and I couldn't find a way out. I knew that sex before marriage was wrong because it was drilled into my head as a teenager. The Bible says in 1 Thessalonians 4:3, "For this is the will of God, even your sanctification that ye should abstain from fornication." Forget having sex before *I* was married, *he* was already married which meant I was committing adultery as well as fornication. It didn't matter which way I looked at it, I was wrapped up in sin like a pig in a blanket. But I couldn't stop seeing him. I knew it was the right thing to do, but my heart wouldn't let me. Somehow I justified staying with him by concluding that he was going to do what he wanted to do anyway; if it wasn't with me, then it would be with someone else.

I was an addict all over again. It was like my first love but more advanced. Reece was a new drug, and I was hooked. I was eighteen, inexperienced, young and playing with the big boys. I thought I could hang, but emotionally and mentally I wasn't even close to being prepared for the next six years of my life.

I continued to see Reece, but now that his wife was in the country, we had to tone things down. I noticed that I couldn't be seen in the passenger seat of his car anymore. I had to duck down until we got off base. I should have been embarrassed and ashamed. I knew I was selling myself short, but I didn't actually believe it. If I saw him, I said something in passing, but we didn't hang out. It was so stupid because everyone knew who he was, and everyone knew I was his girl. Did he really think that people would not remember seeing us after all the time we had spent together and the many times he felt obligated to show me off? Were people talking about me? I'm sure they were. Did I care? I did, but it didn't matter enough to make me stop seeing him.

My best friend tried to talk sense into my head, but she couldn't. When I went home on leave, I showed Mom pictures of Reece and she immediately said that she didn't like him. No one who cared about me seemed to like him for me, yet I couldn't see why they felt that way. They say love is blind, but it's not love that's blind. People choose to ignore rational thought to satisfy lustful desires. Love is many things, none of which are lust.

21

D.Nile Rivers

Reece's wife was never around. She didn't travel in the same circles as I did, and she didn't visit the club, either. I think she came out one time and that's probably because she was checking up on him or wanted to make an appearance so everyone knew that he actually had a wife since no one had ever seen them together; at least not on my base.

Reece was a dog, and I knew it. Everybody knew it. I tried seeing other men, who were interested in me, but they couldn't compare or rather, they just weren't him. So I never pursued anything meaningful with anyone else because I didn't want anyone else. He didn't want me to have anyone else, either. Of course not!

As time went by, we had our ups and downs and our fights. We would make up and start over again. Reece knew exactly what he was doing; whereas, I was still like a child playing catch up in the adult world.

I had unresolved issues from being molested as a child that I didn't know I had. These issues affected my relationship from time to time. I had this thing about control when it came to sex. I was often told that I wasn't open-minded because I just wasn't comfortable doing certain things. I couldn't explain it, and at times it became a problem.

I wasn't conscious of exactly what I did that seemed suspicious or odd to Reece, but my behavior often led to major arguments. I remember sitting in his car one day and Reece putting his hands around my neck and choking me in the midst of one of these arguments. When he let go I slapped him as hard as I could and told him, "You better not ever do that again." That wasn't our last argument. We had others that led to me lying on the hood of his car, like a hood ornament, holding on to his windshield wiper blades as he drove down the street. When he stepped on the brakes I went flying, taking a wiper blade with me.

His car was his passion. He had a Volvo. I don't remember the year, but it was nice. It was burgundy with gold trim and tan leather interior. I knew that all I had to do was mess with his car, and I would get his attention—you play with fire, you will get burn. What I didn't realize was that his car meant more to him than I did.

But even with the fights, I stayed with him. I accepted the fact that he was married and decided that I would never ask him to give up his wife for me. I wanted to seem grown up about it and just take the relationship for what it was. I was beyond shame.

22

Finding Mr. Right

Reece used to say that I would be his forever. I secretly wished it, but didn't say anything about it. I knew that one day we would leave Germany and go our separate ways, but I kept hoping that day would never come.

Chapter Five

Motherhood

I didn't know then, but I know now some twenty years later, that some times when a man wants to keep a woman, he tries to get her pregnant. I still don't understand this concept because they seldom stick around long enough to raise the child or see the pregnancy through. They have a tendency to change their minds and think they can just stop the process of life as if it is no big deal.

Reece had a habit of asking me to have a child for him. I would laugh at him and jokingly wave him off. He would insist that he was serious, and I would always remind him that he was married. Of course, being the player that he was, he had an explanation and a lie for everything and every situation. It was as if he had spent his life writing down "what if" questions and finding the right answers to each one, memorizing them for each situation. I didn't know this at the time. I just took it all in and ate it all up. Whatever he fed me, I ate.

He told me that he couldn't have children. He told me that he was sterile because he and his wife weren't able to have kids. He told me all kinds of stories, at one time or another, until they all kind of ran together and I just didn't know what to believe. But he had a daughter already, so how could he be sterile? He had an answer for that, too.

In August of 1987, before my twentieth birthday, I gave in and agreed to have a baby. I got off birth control and had sex knowing that I could get pregnant. I wasn't thinking anymore. I was wrapped so tightly around Reece's finger that I couldn't even make sense of what I was doing. I didn't think about how it would look when people knew that I was pregnant. I didn't think about how it would affect the child not having his father around because he was married to another woman. I didn't think!!!

Finding Mr. Right

When I got pregnant and told Reece, the response was totally unexpected and devastating. Somewhere along the road to getting me pregnant, he had changed his mind, but didn't tell me. When I told him, he was taken aback. He didn't jump for joy or act excited. He simply remained quiet. He even had the nerve to ask me if it was his. Imagine how I felt! Imagine my disbelief!

Within a week or so, Reece decided that it wasn't the "right" time for me to be pregnant and told me that I should get rid of the baby. Since I was a product of what he had created, and I basically lived to please him, I decided to do what he wanted. I was his puppet, and whatever he did with me and to me was under his control.

I told my boss that I wasn't going to keep the baby. She knew about Reece, and I think she knew about his wife, but I wasn't sure. She took me to a German doctor who explained the abortion procedure to me. I scheduled an appointment and left the clinic in a daze. I walked out of that place not really aware of anything around me or what anyone said. I was there physically, but mentally I was in a whole different world. I kept replaying in my mind and trying to make sense of where I was and how I had gotten there. I kept replaying the conversations in my head that I had had with Reece and the many times he asked me to have his child. I kept trying to understand how, in doing what he wanted, I had upset him to the point where he had changed his mind.

I wanted to please him, but I was scared. I had a decision to make, and I knew that if I didn't make the right decision that I would lose the man who had become my world. But I was so afraid of having the abortion. I had thoughts of trying to fall down the stairs, but I couldn't do it. I even tried jumping up and down, but that didn't work either. All I knew was that I couldn't go through with an abortion. So I decided to keep the baby even if Reece decided he would leave me. My child was more important.

I told Reece that I couldn't do it, and it was a decision that I was making for myself. I told him that I didn't expect anything from him since I was the one making the decision to keep the baby. He wasn't pleased and once I started showing, he stopped seeing me. He didn't want anyone to assume it was his. Funny thing, everybody knew it was.

I went through the pregnancy without him, and to prove a point, he started seeing my roommate who had become my ex-roommate

25

D.Nile Rivers

because I was difficult to get along with now that I was pregnant. I was sick all the time, and I threw up everything I ate. I was just miserable, and I didn't care who else felt it.

Whenever I saw Reece in public, he acted like I didn't exist and would engage in conversation with anyone else around me. I was suffering internally, but at the same time I was bonding with my baby who had now become my world.

I tried to get Reece to visit me in the barracks, but he refused. He didn't even make an effort to check and see how the baby and I were doing.

One night I got up to use the bathroom like I normally did. It was actually early morning around two o'clock. As I walked down the hallway half asleep, I heard Reece's voice coming from my ex-roommate's room. I stopped at the door with my heart in my hand and a hole where it used to be. I didn't need a voice specialist to tell me whose voice I had heard. I had loved this man for the past eighteen months and knew his voice when I heard it. I didn't do anything. I proceeded to the bathroom. I was hurt and very angry. In the midst of my anger I decided that I was going to confront him so that he couldn't deny being with her. On my trip back to my room, I knocked on her door. They stopped speaking and probably hoped that whoever was at the door would leave. I knocked again and this time I told them that I wasn't leaving. I spoke to Reece directly and told him to open the door. I waited. I said, "I know you are in there and if you don't open the door I am going downstairs to report you to the CQ."

The door opened, and Reece came out with a smirk and asked, "What?" as if it were natural and okay for him to be in her room. I couldn't believe the balls on this man. He was good.

I said, "I just wanted you to come out so I could see you for myself, so that you wouldn't have any lies to tell me if I hadn't actually seen you and had accused you of being in the room." With that I turned and went back to my room. I was hurting, and I couldn't hold back the tears. In the midst of my tears, I heard a knock at my door. He came in and tried to explain that he wasn't doing anything and that they were just talking.

"Just talking?" I said. "At two o'clock in the morning?" Of course he had an explanation. He must have checked his list for what to do in this situation and recited the correct answer he had memorized years before. I wasn't buying it, and it didn't matter how he tried to explain

Finding Mr. Right

it. I said, "I'm carrying your child and you can't come to see me, but you can come to see her?" He tried to speak, but I had nothing else to say.

He knew I couldn't stand my ex-roommate, and to find him with her was more than I could take. It didn't matter what he had to say at that point.

I was alone and I was not dealing with things well. My best friend had already left Germany and so had Fran. Fran had gotten pregnant on purpose in order to get discharged from the military. I didn't have anyone there that I was really close to. I wasn't able to speak about the pregnancy because it was *supposed* to be a secret. I didn't have anyone to blame but myself and I wasn't getting any sympathy either. I didn't deserve it any way. I should have known better.

At some point during my pregnancy, I became friends with a girl in my unit. Cindy lived in housing with her husband, and as we became good friends, she invited me to stay with them. I didn't want to accept, but I didn't want to be alone. Near the end of my pregnancy, I moved in with her. She agreed to be my coach in the delivery room seeing that I had no one else. Cindy also helped me get housing off base and a car.

On the night I went into labor, I was awakened from a deep sleep by an incredibly sharp pain in my abdomen. I didn't know what labor felt like, but I had an idea that it was something like what I was experiencing. I woke Cindy up and told her, but because we didn't want to go to the hospital and have them send me back home because my cervix wasn't dilated, we decided that we would wait. I tried to go back to sleep but it happened again. I decided to take a walk to help bring the labor along. I told Cindy that I was going for a walk and left the house. I walked about fifteen minutes to my apartment in housing. On the way there, I kept feeling like I had to use the bathroom. I stopped a few times and urinated in the bushes along the way, but when I finally got to my apartment, I just felt the need to defecate. It wasn't that I had to go, I just felt like it.

While I was there dealing with my bathroom issues, I heard a knock at the door. It was Cindy. She had followed me in her car just in case I needed to get to the hospital. I was glad that she had because the contractions were closer to five minutes apart and I couldn't walk back.

She got me into the car, and we went to the hospital. When I got there, they told me that I was in the wrong place and that they were

D.Nile Rivers

full. But prior to sending me on my way, the doctor did an exam to determine how dilated my cervix was and I almost kicked her because of the pain she caused me. I couldn't believe she stuck her hand inside me like it was nothing. I was angry. I was already in pain and dealing with it like a trooper. Here she came along and made it worse. I was heated!

But dilated or not, we couldn't stay there. She told Cindy that I would have to go to Frankfurt, which was almost an hour away. I was not happy because the contractions had gotten even closer together. It didn't matter. They put me in an ambulance and slowly drove to Frankfurt. I was even more heated. They didn't put the sirens on, but had the lights flashing. I guess they didn't see the urgency in getting me there. All I knew was that I was in extreme pain and I wanted something to make the pain go away.

Cindy wasn't allowed in the ambulance with me so she followed along in her car. I told her to try and contact Reece so he could be there, but he never came. He couldn't. What did I expect? Did I really think that he would want to be there? Yes, I did.

I held on to the hand of the paramedic, and I knew she wished I hadn't. Every time a contraction hit me, I squeezed her hand for dear life. The contractions were coming once every other minute, but even knowing that, they still didn't see the urgency in driving faster.

When I finally got to the hospital, the doctor on duty felt the urgency of the situation and immediately took me away. She took good care of me and saw to it that I got what I needed. She told me that she was going to give me an epidural. Once she told me that it would numb me, I was all for it. She told me it would hurt when they stuck the needle in my back, but I didn't feel a thing. The needle was nothing compared to the contractions I was having. Once they did the epidural, I told them to take all the time that they needed because I wasn't feeling a thing. When they wheeled me into the delivery room to perform my surgery (c-section), Cindy decided to wait outside. All of a sudden she wasn't feeling up to it. I didn't mind.

I was tired and wanted nothing more than to go to sleep, but I wanted to stay awake long enough to see my baby. I wanted a boy. I wanted him to look just like his father, and that is exactly what I got.

When he came out, he had a cone head and for days I called him Conan. I didn't have a name for him, so they put my last name on the band around his arm. I had a name all picked out, but when I saw him

28

Finding Mr. Right

it just didn't seem to fit.

He was born between three and four in the morning weighing eight pounds and thirteen ounces. He was healthy, had a nice set of lungs, looked like his dad, and I was relieved. It was time for me to sleep.

When I woke up, I wished that I hadn't. A nurse came to me and told me that I had to get out of the bed and walk around. I asked her if she was crazy, but she was probably used to that reaction from women. I had just had my stomach cut open and she wanted me to get up and walk. I really thought she needed to get her head examined. I ignored her, hoping she would go away. I tried to go back to sleep. She left, but came back a while later.

When I finally agreed to get up, I felt like my stomach had hit the floor. It was even more painful than the contractions. All I wanted to do was get back in the bed. The nurse had every explanation why I had to get up. Maybe she and Reece had gone to the same school of explanations and answers. Anyway, I finally did what she wanted and quickly got back in bed.

Reece came to see me later on in the day. Surprisingly enough, he had something to say about my stomach. He asked, "That's going to go down right?" I couldn't believe him. I had just given birth and he wanted me to look like I hadn't been pregnant for the past forty weeks. Yet I still stayed with him.

I got phone calls from people I knew, but I couldn't give them a name when they asked. Finally, my Commander (the officer in charge of my unit) gave me a name, Trey, and I added the rest. I remained in the hospital for five days so that they could monitor the baby and me. I didn't want to be there, but they knew best. Besides, I didn't know the first thing about being a mother, and a single parent at that.

When I got home from the hospital, one of the first things I did was get on the floor and try to do sit ups. I couldn't do one! I was so upset. I went from being in the gym and being in shape to not being able to do one sit up. I was trying to make my stomach flatter because Reece had made a comment about it. Did it matter to me that I had just had surgery and the muscles in my stomach had been cut? Did it matter that I was in pain, but trying to ignore it so that I could work on my body to please this man? No! I was still allowing him to pull my strings and somehow I had convinced myself that it was right. I still had a lot to learn.

Not only was I unable to do a sit up, but I also couldn't believe

29

D.Nile Rivers

how ugly my stomach had become from being pregnant. I didn't realize I had stretch marks until I had delivered Trey. My stomach was so hideous that I couldn't look at myself in the mirror. I didn't think anyone else would ever want to look at me again either. I concluded that each stretch mark was a reminder of my sins.

As it turned out, I had an apartment down the street from Reece. Not a good thing, but it didn't really matter because he wasn't speaking to me. That is what I thought until he came over one day. I guess it was all right to see me because all of a sudden he was back in my life now that I was no longer pregnant. Somehow he felt this would make a difference to the people who knew me and knew that he was the father. I never did understand his justification of how he treated me when I was pregnant; maybe it had something to do with the fact that I took him back.

I didn't know what I expected. Things weren't the way they used to be. We didn't hang out at the clubs or anything like that. I had a responsibility now, and I didn't have time to be in the club the way I used to be. Instead, I spent the majority of my time working my regular hours and hanging out with other people who had children. I had a girlfriend, Jackie, who lived a couple apartments over from where I lived. She was a single mother as well, and we helped each other out whenever possible.

It was a struggle for me at first, trying to find good daycare providers, and it didn't help that I had to leave for training a month after I had Trey. I had to go away for two weeks and finding someone to take care of him was a chore, but more than that, I didn't want to leave my baby so soon. But you don't really have a choice when the military orders you to go. You just go!

It would have been nice if I could have had Reece take care of him or even look out for him, but that wasn't a possibility. Even though he came over to visit whenever he felt like it, it wasn't for anything other than to have sex with me. He didn't claim the baby. There wasn't any family outing or anything like that. We didn't walk around like we were a couple or anything. I didn't expect anything more than what I had. I had made the decision and I was going to take care of my child by myself.

I thought I knew what I was doing, but I didn't. My decision to get pregnant, in order to please Reece was a major mistake. My first mistake was having sex to begin with. My second mistake was staying

Finding Mr. Right

involved with Reece once I knew he was married. The third mistake was agreeing to have his child knowing he was married and wouldn't be there for the child. My choices were all selfish; I was trying to please myself by getting what I wanted no matter what it took to get it. I didn't think about how the child would feel growing up without a father. I didn't think past the baby years and how cute he would be. I didn't think about the struggles associated with being a single parent.

My decision caused a lot of anger and hurt in a child who didn't ask to be here. It took me years to realize this. For years I struggled with resentment. I resented the fact that I was foolish enough to get involved the way I did. I resented the fact that, after all I did for him, I was nothing more than a roll in the hay.

Chapter Six

A Woman Scorned

My ordeal of a relationship with Reece left me bitter. I swore to myself that I would never mess with a married man again, and I meant to keep that vow. I was ashamed of what I had done. I had grown from my experience, and I was no longer as naïve as I used to be. I was taking responsibility for my own actions, and I wasn't going to let another man turn me into his puppet ever again. We'll see about that.

Reece wasn't the only married man that tried to be with me; I just never got involved again. The opportunities were there and limitless, but I had my wits about me, and I didn't want to go down that road again. But you just never knew who was married.

Being with Reece taught me that you couldn't tell a married man just by looking at him. If he was out trying to pick up a woman, chances are, he wasn't going to act like he was married (One of the things the church didn't teach me.). So, I became very skeptical and very cold. I didn't trust men and that was all right with me because I wasn't over Reece anyway.

I grew numb towards men, and it showed. If a man tried to talk to me the first thing out of my mouth was, "Are you married?" The next question was usually, "You want to screw me, don't you?"

It was always priceless to see their expression when I asked that question. They usually stumbled over their words and would say, "Well, uh, yes, eventually."

Then I would say, "That's what I thought" and would walk away and leave them standing there with their mouths open. I didn't care because I wasn't interested. I was disgusted and angry because I had been hurt. Not only was I deceived to begin with, but I was also deceived long enough to fall in love so deeply that I did whatever he

32

Finding Mr. Right

wanted (the devil and his tricks). I kicked myself for a long time after what I had gotten myself into, and I was now at a point where I wasn't up to dealing with any more games unless I was in charge. I didn't have time to beat around the bush. I realized what men were about, and I wasn't just something for them to use when they felt like it.

By this time, I had been around military men long enough to learn their habits and their games. Once I had Trey, Reece wasn't around like he used to be, which meant I had a lot of free time. I wasn't that same girl, spending time sitting in the window looking for him to pass by or holding my breath waiting in my room and hoping he would call. I still felt like I was his, but it didn't stop me from getting my flirt on. He had basically left me on my own, so men thought I was available.

I had grown some and done my research. At work I hung out with guys and listened to the conversations they had with each other. I learned the reasons behind why they cheated on their wives and girlfriends. I learned their habits and the games they played. Once I had enough research, I decided to go into business for myself, so to speak. I was tired of being hurt by men, so I decided to flip the switch. I became like them.

I played the same games they played on women. If I came across a man I was interested in, I lured him along and then dismissed him like he was nothing, especially if I caught his game. I got good at detecting game within the first few minutes of a conversation. If the conversation was somewhat interesting and the guy was cute, I entertained him until I got bored. If the conversation was all about sex within the first few minutes or if he couldn't keep his eyes above my chest, then he felt my wrath. Did I have it like that? Apparently so because that's what I did, and it didn't deter them; they just kept coming.

There was only one man that I was tempted to get involved with other than Reece while I was there. He was gorgeous, even more so than Reece. But he was married. He was a really nice guy and nice to talk to, but when I found out that he was married, I told him, "I respect you too much to do that to you." It would have been very easy for me to get involved with him, but we probably both would have fallen for each other, and I couldn't do that to him or his wife. It was difficult turning him down, but I couldn't see myself going there again. I had to pat myself on the back for that one because even in the midst of my scorn, I was able to have some kind of feelings. I had a bad taste in my mouth towards men who cheated, but there was just something about

D.Nile Rivers

this one that brought out some sort of emotion besides anger and hatred.

My behavior towards men started rumors about me. My lack of interest in them was an insult to their egos. They spread rumors that I wasn't into men. I thought it was funny, but people who knew me ignored the gossip. It didn't matter to me one way or the other. They also started other rumors that eventually got around to Reece. Someone thought he was funny and went around bragging about how he had me. It wasn't true, but it got back to Reece and he confronted me about it. Mind you, this man had three women at the same time, and he had the nerve to confront me! He didn't want me any more, but no one else could have me either. Yeah, he had a lot of nerve.

Germany was an experience I will never forget. I was there for three years and eight months. When I left in April, 1989, I took my experiences and the lessons learned with me. What exactly did I learn? That I had no idea what I was doing.

Finding Mr. Right

Chapter Seven

The Real World

Once I got back home, with the help of Mom, things became bearable. I actually had hopes that I could be a single parent. I was healthy, strong, surrounded by people who loved me, and I was going to be all right; except, I wasn't all right. Physically I was fine, but emotionally I was withdrawn. I had my own room, and I made sure I had everything I needed in it (everything I was allowed to have in it) so that I didn't have to come out unless it was absolutely necessary. I didn't stay in there all of the time, but for the majority of the time, that is where I stayed. I had my son, my weights, and my music. I didn't really need much more than that.

I didn't think about whether my actions were affecting anyone else in the house. No one really said much. I think they just accepted me for who I was and let me be. I didn't want to be hugged or fussed over. I didn't want anyone touching me unless they had permission. That's just where I was at the time.

Nobody understood why I was that way. The sad thing, I didn't even know why I was that way. Mom always said that I was such a loving and happy child, but I didn't know that child she spoke of.

I got a job working as a temp in the Department of Social Services. My plan was to save as much money as I could so that I could move to Texas to be with Reece. He called me when he got to the States (which wasn't long after I had arrived) to let me know where he was, and every four months when I just couldn't suppress my hormones, I went to see him. Even with the distance between us, I was still his girl. I wasn't seeing anyone and still had no interest in doing so.

Reece asked me to move to Texas to be with him, and because I was still strung out over him, I agreed. Once I had enough money

35

D.Nile Rivers

saved up, I got on a plane and went to El Paso, Texas. Mom agreed to keep Trey for me for a month while I tried to find work. Reece found me a furnished apartment and that's where I stayed.

Getting used to the hundred and ten degree temperature was something that took adjusting to. I didn't know what Texas was like, but I definitely didn't expect what I got. I got headaches for a week until I adjusted. I wasn't used to air conditioning, but it quickly became my friend.

I thought finding a job would have been easy, but it wasn't. I couldn't find a job anywhere. I couldn't even get a job at Burger King. It was horrible. I ended up getting a job selling perfume. We had to buy the product and we made our money based on how much we sold. I wasn't and still am not a sales person. I have never been able to sell or force someone to buy something they didn't want. But I needed a job in order to provide for Trey and myself. Once I had that job, I went home and brought Trey back with me.

My girlfriend from Germany, Jackie, who had lived next door to me in the housing, lived in Texas as well, so I had someone there I knew besides Reece. She and I spent time hanging out together. While she took me around and showed me a good time, I found that I had spent all the money I had. It didn't take long for me to realize that the job I had pedaling perfume wasn't working for me. If they said, "No" then it was simply that, which meant I wasn't making any money.

When the money ran out, I tried to get on welfare. I didn't know what else to do, and I didn't want to go back home. I didn't ask Reece for money either. Instead, I called home and borrowed money from a close friend of mine.

I didn't see Reece as much as I would have liked, but he came by when he felt like it. We didn't hang out in public like we were an item or anything, and when I did see him in public, I spent the majority of the time trying to keep Trey from saying, "Daddy." It was embarrassing and hurtful, but it was part of the consequences I hadn't thought about before getting pregnant. This wasn't the first time.

There was a time in Germany, when we were at one of Reece's basketball games, when Trey saw Reece and tried to call out to him. Reece's wife just happened to be sitting in the bleachers almost directly behind me. This was the first time I realized the world I brought my son into. I never thought ahead when he had asked me to get pregnant; I simply wanted to please him.

Finding Mr. Right

One day I went to a softball game to watch Reece play. He got injured during the game, and it was only natural that I would be concerned. His wife was also at the game. I didn't know.

I found out what hospital he was taken to and went to find him. When I found what room he was in, I walked in without thinking and was surprised to find them both in the room. You should have seen the look on his face. It was priceless. I don't know if she caught on, but I played it off. I said, "Hey Reece, I was in the hospital visiting a friend and I heard you had gotten hurt." Now even I wouldn't have believed that. I made idle conversation for a few minutes and wished him well. On my way out the door, his wife asked, "Do I know you? You look so familiar." I said, "I was stationed in Germany years ago and I knew Reece from back then." We talked a little more, and then I left stating that I was going to visit my girlfriend who was also in the hospital. That was close.

I got a mouthful from Reece later on. I got chewed out for almost blowing his cover. But he explained his way out of it and either she believed it or just didn't care.

Reece and I were on one minute and off the next. I wanted more of his time and he didn't have it to give. One thing led to another, and I would get upset and threaten to do damage to his most prized possession, his car. He had the same Volvo that he had in Germany. He had it shipped when he came to the States.

Well, I guess I hadn't learned not to mess with his car because in the midst of an argument one night, I threw some tiny rocks at his car, and the next thing I knew I was up against a stone wall with his hands around my throat. I had forgotten that the car meant more to him than me. When I was able to get away from him and into the house, he came through the door, and I had a knife. Trey had found a closet to hide in and was crying. Reece got the knife away from me and I threw a tantrum, throwing things around the apartment.

We normally made up after a fight, but this time was different. And even though I had enough of dealing with Reece, I didn't want to go back home. The money I had borrowed was just about gone. I didn't want to ask Reece for money, but I knew I had to do something.

I swallowed my pride, and I got up one morning while it was still dark, wrapped Trey up in a blanket and walked to the welfare office. It was about an hour walk, and I spent most of it crying because Trey was so heavy and he couldn't walk the distance we had to travel. When I

D.Nile Rivers

got there, they told me that I wasn't eligible for welfare. I couldn't believe my ears. It hit me hard! I didn't know what I was going to do. As I walked out of that office broken and at my wits end, I cried as I picked Trey up and made my way back to the apartment. I still had no idea what I was going to do. I was desperate.

The next morning, as I watched television in my bedroom, a preacher on the television asked if I wanted to be saved. He said that Jesus Christ was the answer and that he would supply all my needs. I had nothing more to lose, and everything to gain. I fell to my knees and cried out to God. I was as low as I'd ever been, and with very little hope. I needed help. I did what the preacher said and repeated the sinner's prayer as he said it. I repented of my sins and believed that things would be different. When I got up from the floor, I made the decision that I would go back to Massachusetts and start my life over. I called Jackie, and she came over and gave me the money for a bus ticket home. I packed up my things, contacted Reece and asked him if he would put my things in storage until I could have them sent to me.

When I got back to Massachusetts, things were different. I had a new outlook on life and my faith in God. I was able to land three jobs when I couldn't even find one in Texas. I worked in retail at the mall, did security at night for apartment buildings, and started drilling with the Army Reserves again. God was making changes in my life and things were great. I wanted to do the right thing and live according to the Word of God. I knew that meant I would have to let Reece go, and I did. At least I thought I did.

Chapter Eight

Lust at First Sight

Life was going well. I was happy and in love with Jesus. This lasted for a while until my hormones kicked in and I started having sex again. I really tried to be good, but my body was craving sex like an addict. I would be fine for a while and then somewhere around the four-month mark, I would need a fix. I couldn't live like this, I couldn't be a hypocrite. I wanted to live according to God's Word, but I couldn't control my need for sex, and I was too ashamed to talk to someone in the church about it. I had so much to learn about being saved. I didn't understand about being weak and the constant cravings of my flesh; the battle between doing right, and doing wrong. I didn't know that it was the devil's job to try to make me feel that God wouldn't forgive me for messing up; to try and persuade me to go back to living in sin. Because I didn't know, I stopped going to church and decided that since I couldn't live right all the time that I would just be bad all the time.

If I had known more about God, I would have known that the Bible says in Romans 8:1, "There is therefore now no condemnation to them which are in Christ Jesus, who walk not after the flesh, but after the Spirit." I would have known that what I was experiencing was already mentioned in Galatians 5:17 where it says, "For the flesh lusteth against the Spirit, and the Spirit against the flesh: and these are contrary the one to the other: so that ye cannot do the things that ye would." In other words, I would have known that there would always be a conflict between my spirit and my flesh when it came to making choices between good and bad. I was still a babe in my Christian walk, and the enemy was trying to get me back. He was using my old ways and desires to tempt me to mess up. It worked because I didn't know

D.Nile Rivers

the Bible well enough, and because I hadn't received enough teaching about God, His love and His forgiveness. As a result, I gave in to my flesh and went back to what I knew, a life in sin. The enemy was waiting with open arms to welcome me back. He had numerous prospects and opportunities waiting to satisfy my sexual needs.

It seemed like it was always easy for me to attract someone, but I was never the girlfriend type. Even when I thought I was, I would learn that there was somebody else on the side or I was the girl on the side.

I met a guy through a bus driver friend of mine. After riding the same bus back and forth to the mall for work, I struck up a relationship with a bus driver. He was cute and all, but not my type. One day he told me that he had a friend he thought I would like and he wanted me to meet him. I asked him to describe him. He seemed to fit the bill. I called him, and he and I got to know each other over the phone. He didn't want us to meet right away. He told me that he wanted to get himself in shape first because he knew the kind of guys that I was attracted to. By the time we met, it didn't matter what he looked like because we had gotten to know each other to the point where I liked him for what I knew of him, not what he looked like.

Our first meeting was at my house. Floyd showed up tall, large, dark, and cute. He was six feet and four inches tall, and weighed over two hundred pounds, but his weight was well proportioned to his build. I was pleased. He was pleased with the way I looked, as well. I wasn't exactly what he had pictured. He didn't realize that when I told him I worked out that I was for real and not some girl who went to the gym to look at guys. So we were both pleased.

Not too long after he and I hooked up, he told me about his ex-girlfriend and how jealous she was. I was not in the mood for any ex-girlfriend drama and wanted it to stay far from me. I had already dealt with enough drama in my life. He told me stories of how she wanted him back and because he was no longer interested (so he said) she did all sorts of things to his car and harassed him on a regular basis.

After a few months of being with Floyd, he showed up at my house one night. He asked if he could stay with me (something he never did because I was living at Mom's house) and I told him that he could. I was still asleep, and didn't really pay much attention to him. He left in the morning and said that he would call me later.

Later that morning I got a visit from some police detectives asking

Finding Mr. Right

me questions about Floyd. I was totally at a loss for words. They wanted to know if he was with me the night before, and I told them that he had been. When I asked them what it was about, they didn't tell me.

When Floyd called me later that day, he told me that the police were looking for him. I couldn't believe it. I was in shock. He explained that he and his ex-girlfriend had an argument the day before because he was sick and tired of her harassing him. He said that he went over to her house, and they got into a fight where he almost strangled her. So she called the cops on him. In my mind, I thought, if she's still alive then that's not murder. There was more. Apparently his former girlfriend (the one before the ex) had been strangled with a telephone cord in her house that same day. It got better! Floyd confessed to me that he had gone to see her and that they had gotten intimate. He said that she sent him to the store and when he came back she was dead. He said that he didn't hang around because he didn't want anyone to blame it on him. I believed him. I tried to make sense of all he had said, but it wasn't making any sense. Apparently, the cops felt that because he had tried to strangle his ex-girlfriend that there was a pattern and he was the most likely suspect for the murder.

Floyd went to jail and was there for over two years for a murder he didn't commit. I went to see Floyd whenever I could, but he eventually got moved to another facility. We wrote each other often, but at some point we just lost touch. After being in jail for almost two years, I read in the newspaper that they had found the individual who had actually murdered the girl, and even though Floyd was innocent of the murder charge, he was being kept in jail for attempted murder of his ex-girlfriend.

I had never been involved in anything like this before, so I was full of questions and even more, I was upset because I hadn't had enough time with Floyd. But I guess I shouldn't have been too upset because like so many other men I knew, he wasn't faithful, either.

Because of this event in my life, I enrolled in college to get a law enforcement degree. I felt that Floyd had been held in jail awaiting trial longer than necessary and against his rights. I couldn't understand how the system could be so prejudiced (I was still ignorant to many things in life). Based on Floyd's case, I also decided that I wanted to get a law degree so that I could defend the innocent.

I started college full-time in the spring of 1991. It was great! In order to support Trey and myself, I became a school bus driver, which worked out perfectly. I drove the kids to school in the mornings and then I went to my classes. When I was through with classes for the day, it was usually right around the time to pick up the kids from school. I drove the bus during the day and did security at night.

When school was out for the summer months, I volunteered to go on active duty status with the military. When I had returned to Massachusetts from Germany, I had enlisted with the Army Reserve to finish out my goal of serving twenty years in the military. My active duty tour was at Devens which was an hour and fifteen minutes north of where I lived. I was only able to do this because Mom agreed to watch Trey while I was away making money. I didn't think of it then, but it was very selfish of me to leave Trey with her while I was off having fun. Sure, I was working, but I was having fun as well.

Being on active duty in the summer was great fun. I got to work during the day and have fun at night. I got to meet all kinds of men and made all sorts of friends while I was there.

Once again, I was new meat and the dogs were out, but I was a little wiser now. Reece had taught me a lot, and at this point I knew all about the game and was able to play by my own rules.

I landed a job working for an intelligence unit at Devens during the summer months as administrative help. I had my own suite, was paid active duty pay, and had active duty benefits.

During my first summer there in 1990, I had the opportunity to learn the ins and outs of the base, the units, the men, what clubs to go to, etc. I made some female friends and because they lived in the area all year, they were able to take me around. I didn't have a car so I was dependent on others to get where I needed to go.

Once the tour was over, I was able to go back to my job as a bus driver every year. But after the first year, the base downsized and shipped the active duty personnel to various parts of the world. The base was now a Reserve base and had very little activity. In the first year I was there, it was all good. I had a blast being new and getting all the attention. I decided to try out the games I had learned from watching and listening to the men I had hung out with in Germany.

It wasn't unusual for me to have more than one date in a night. I would make plans and space them out so that the dates didn't overlap. The only problem was, the men I was interested in were all in the same unit, so I had to be smart about how I went about my game. I was playing a really serious game talking to men in the same unit because

Finding Mr. Right

men talk and word would get around. But I knew the ones I wanted to talk to and those I didn't. So for the ones I liked, they knew it.

I was smart enough to know that even though I was interested in these men, I wasn't going to sleep with them. I didn't mind being labeled a flirt, but I wasn't trying to be called a whore. They might even have called me a tease, but that was because they didn't get what they wanted. There's an art to flirting without being a tease; at least that's how I saw it.

We all had fun. I hung out with some of the ladies I had befriended on the base. The only problem I had with my female friends was their husbands always flirting with me. I considered myself being polite, but for some reason they always felt the need to try to hook up with me behind their wives' backs. I never told their wives. If I felt one of their husbands trying to be too friendly with me, I stopped going to their house and made sure I was never alone with them.

There was always somewhere to go for a party and there were usually the same group of guys there, many of whom I was interested in, but because I was just flirting and not serious about any of them, this was usually the only time I saw them. We had fun on the dance floor. It was usually a time when we would all get hot and bothered from dancing, but that's where it stayed, on the dance floor.

I can remember one time when I almost got busted and realized that I really had to be a little better at my game. I sent a message to one of the guys I was interested in by another guy I knew that hung out with him. The message was for him to come by my suite. Well, when I heard a knock at my door expecting Tony, I was shocked to see Terry instead. I had gotten the names mixed up and sent the message to the wrong guy. I played it off, and let Terry in because I liked him, too (He reminded me of Reece). Terry thought he looked like Malcolm X. He even wore glasses that made him resemble Malcolm. Like guys do, Terry ran his mouth about seeing me to one of his friends not realizing that his friend liked me. As a result, this friend of his, who I enjoyed hanging out with when we went dancing, decided that he didn't want to speak to me after that. I didn't mind too much because I didn't like him in that way, anyway.

The summer of 1992 at Devens, is a summer I will never forget. It was during this summer that I met my idea of "Mr. Right." The base was no longer active, and all the people I had known from the year before were all gone. There was hardly anybody on base or anyone to speak to. So the only people to hang out with were the ones in the unit I was working for (the intelligence school) or the students who came through the school for training.

I worked as one of the clerks designated to in-process the students. I had access to all their personal data, so I was able to determine who was married and who wasn't, etc. Summer was almost over and no one had come through that I could flirt with. Here it was, the last class cycle, and I needed some excitement.

In-processing day came and I noticed, while looking through the files, that one of the students had a birthday that was the day after mine. I also noticed that he was married and he was an officer. Enlisted soldiers weren't supposed to mingle outside their rank. I made a mental note and decided that I would just wish him a happy birthday when I met him. It was all part of my flirting charm.

I didn't know what he looked like, and I really wasn't looking for a man because it was almost time to go back home and sadly enough, this was also the year I turned twenty-five. I had made a promise to Reece that if we were both single when I turned twenty-five, that I would look him up. Fortunately for me, something happened that summer at Devens.

As I sat in my assigned area, I waited for the students to arrive so I could process them in. There was no set time for them to arrive so there were moments throughout the day when there was nothing to do. When a student arrived, I took their information and gave them whatever materials they needed for their various classes.

Things were pretty boring for the majority of the day. I hadn't met any one I wanted to flirt with and things were looking pretty bleak until I looked down the hallway and saw a man walking towards me. He caught my attention. I didn't know who he was, but I knew I wanted to get to know him. He had on shorts, and a t-shirt. He was chocolate and fine! He had big arms, big legs, nice calves, a nice muscular chest, and a wide back. He was just my cup of tea. Yummy!

When he finally got to my table, I played it cool. I couldn't show that I was interested. The way he looked, he probably got a lot of attention, and I wanted to appear as uninterested as possible.

I did his paperwork and struck up a little conversation with him. He was as much of a flirt as I was. When I saw his name, I realized that he was the same student I had looked up earlier with the birthday the day after mine. I couldn't believe it, but I also remembered that his

Finding Mr. Right

records stated that he was married. What a disappointment!

As we both flirted with each other and made idle conversation, he asked about the gym on base. I mentioned to him that I went to the gym daily. I could tell he was making a mental note of that. He couldn't really tell what I looked like under the uniform I was wearing so it was a bit of a mystery to him. He asked for directions to the gym, and I was more than happy to give them to him. I hadn't forgotten the information about him being married which was in the back of my mind. We were just playing the flirting game. He mentioned that he liked to run and maybe he would see me at the gym later. Before he left I said, "Happy early birthday." He turned around and looked at me. I said, "Your birthday is the day after mine." He smiled and thanked me on the way out.

After I got released from duty that day, I rode my bike to the gym like I normally did. I was hoping I would run into him, but even if I didn't, I was certain I would run into him within the two week period that he was at the school.

I had time to finish my workout and I still hadn't seen him. I was a little disappointed. I left the gym and got on my bike, ready to go back to my room. As I was leaving, I saw him jogging towards the building. I rode out to meet him. I smiled and said, "Hi, Sir." He asked if I wanted to ride along with him as he jogged. Well, I just couldn't resist. I wanted to be around him as much as possible. I was like a bee drawn to honey.

As he jogged, I rode and we talked. I learned that he was separated from his wife and going through a divorce. He said that he had three children and he was a New York police officer. He was also a helicopter pilot in the Army Reserves. And to top all that off, he was fine! What a package!

By the time I heard that he was going through a divorce and was separated, I was already wishing and hoping that he was as interested in me as much as I was in him. I put my *best* game forward and by the time he was through with his run, he knew where I was staying, the phone number to the pay phone on my floor, and everything else he needed to know.

D.Nile Rivers

Chapter Nine

It's On

I reluctantly left him and went back to my suite. I couldn't stop thinking about him. I was so excited when I got a knock on my door later on that night telling me that I had a phone call down the hall (we didn't have phones in our rooms). I didn't need to pretend to be cool while walking to the phone because he wasn't there to see my excitement, but when I said hello, I pretended like it was no big deal and that I hadn't been hoping he would call. We continued our conversation from where we left off earlier in the day and by the end of the conversation, things were looking very positive.

The next day was orientation for the students. They were all instructed to meet in the auditorium. I had my eye open for Chief to show up. I called him Chief because of his rank. He was a Chief Warrant Officer. He saw me first and commented on my hairstyle. It wasn't anything fancy to me, but he was that kind of guy; he noticed your hair, your clothes, and he especially liked shoes. That was a first for me.

Because he was in classes during the day and I was in the office working, I didn't see him again until lunch. Since he was an officer and I was an enlisted sergeant, we weren't supposed to mingle. When I saw him during lunch, I smiled as I tried to keep my interest in him on the down low. I didn't want to get either one of us in trouble for fraternizing. I wasn't allowed to sit with him or even talk to him on a personal level unless it involved work.

After work I went to the gym, and when I returned to my room, I received a call from Chief. I invited him to come over. He accepted and I couldn't get off the phone fast enough to get myself ready for his visit.

46

Finding Mr. Right

My room was always clean, so I didn't have any cleaning to do in preparation for his visit. All I wanted to make sure was straight, was me. But I had to make sure I didn't appear eager or desperate when he arrived. I didn't want him to think that my sole purpose for him coming over was because I wanted him, even though I could sense the feeling was mutual.

When I heard the knock on my door, I took my time responding, and when I opened the door and saw him standing there, it was all over. I invited him in and we chilled for a bit. I won't get into details, but he stayed the night and the next and the next. He stayed in my room for the entire two weeks he was there. It was the best two weeks I ever spent at Devens.

I continued working as usual, making sure not to breathe a word to anyone. He kept going to class and at the end of the day, he would slip into my room without anyone seeing. He told me that his fellow officers were questioning him about where he was staying, but he made something up. We enjoyed each other's company the entire time, and what made it more exciting was the fact that no one knew.

I even went out to the club one night and met up with one of his classmates, a lieutenant. He was cute and everything, but I was so not into him. My mind was back at the base and in my room wishing I was with Chief and not in the club. But I kept up the game and pretended to enjoy myself.

I couldn't wait to leave the club. The first opportunity I got, I left. When I slipped into the room and stood by the side of the bed to see if Chief was asleep, he looked at me and said, "It's about time."

I said, "I've been thinking about you the entire time. I wanted to leave, but I couldn't." He understood and said that he had thought of me being with the lieutenant and didn't like what he was thinking. It felt good to have someone waiting on me. He said he wasn't used to it, but that it was nice waiting for my return.

The day Chief had to leave was a very difficult day for me. Not only was it a problem trying to see him before he left, but I had to try to talk to him without having anyone see us. I finally caught up to him and as he spoke to me, I just wanted to cry. I felt like a part of me was dying inside, and I thought I was actually going to die, but he reassured me that we would see each other again. He kissed me and pulled himself away. When I went back to the office all eyes were on me. I finally broke my cover and explained that he and I had been seeing

D.Nile Rivers

each other. The girls were happy for me and intrigued with the love story.

Throughout the day, I kept telling them how much I didn't want him to go. I guess they got tired of hearing it because one of the girls let me borrow her car, and I got permission to leave the next day for the weekend. I called Chief and told him the good news. He was excited.

Chief lived about three hours away from Devens. I didn't care. He could have lived on the moon. I drove there with anticipation the entire way. He had to work the entire weekend so our time together would be limited, but all that mattered to me was that I would get to see him. If it was just a few minutes a day, I would take it.

When I got to the location where we were supposed to meet, he pulled up in his police cruiser and told me to follow him. When we got there, he jumped out of his car. I got out of mine. I tried to be cool, but he was way beyond that stage of the game. He quickly propped me up against the building and kissed me like only he could. He had the ability to kiss me for long periods of time without needing to breathe. I had to stop him so I could get air. He laughed. He put the true meaning in the phrase "take your breath away." He was happy to see me and didn't have a problem expressing his glee. But I wasn't used to this kind of genuine affection and didn't respond in kind. I held back a little, and he looked at me strangely. I played it off as though I was just tired from the drive. He was too excited to see me to be bothered. He was still on the clock, so he made sure that I got settled in to his place and went back to work.

While he was at work the next day, I shopped for some presents. I bought him roses and lingerie. When he came home from work he was pleasantly surprised. He said he had never gotten roses before. I was glad. We made love and the rest is history.

The weekend went by faster than either of us wanted and sooner than I wanted, I headed back to Devens to finish my tour of duty for the summer. He and I stayed in touch the rest of my time there and when it was time for me to go back home, he offered to pick me up and give me a ride. It was a good feeling to have a man actually go out of his way to do something for me. Reece was nothing like that.

Chief was true to his word. When my time was up, he came and picked me up and gave me a ride home.

During the ride home I kept hoping time would stand still, but of

Finding Mr. Right

course that only happens in the movies. Instead of the ride taking an hour and fifteen minutes, it took about fifty. He was just used to driving fast.

Chief and my son hit it off and Mom seemed to like him. Unfortunately, he couldn't stay very long because he had a long drive back, but the time was well spent.

We saw each other whenever we could until May of 1993 when I graduated from college. The plan was for him to come to my graduation, and he didn't. It broke my heart. My family had a graduation party for me, and I ended up in bed crying myself to sleep. I just felt that it was an important occasion in my life, and I wanted him to be there. Instead, my boss, who had been hitting on me since we met, showed up driving a limousine with a dozen roses to save the day. I was impressed and grateful, but it just wasn't the same. When I finally spoke to Chief, he told me that he was unable to get away from work and he was sorry he wasn't there. I believed him because I knew he was always working. I understood his financial problems, but I also knew that I needed more.

As perfect as Chief was, I knew he had his faults. He even asked me to have a child for him. I laughed it off because I didn't think he was serious. Besides, it struck me as the "I want to hold on to you for life" tactic. The same one Reece had played on me. So I brushed it off as a joke.

A few months after my graduation, nothing had changed. Chief was still constantly working and it seemed like every conversation we had always led to his issues regarding the lack of money. I felt badly for him, but there was nothing I could do to help. I was already doing my best to provide for Trey and myself. The more Chief and I spoke, the more I realized that I needed more from him and he wasn't in the position to give me what I needed. I needed to spend time with him and he didn't have it. It wouldn't have been a problem for me to go see him, but because he had no time to himself, there was no time to speak of. I knew I had to let Chief go. He had enough to deal with and didn't need me constantly bothering him about spending time with him.

Breaking up with him hit me like a ton of bricks. I spent numerous hours crying in bed. Letting go of him literally broke my heart. At times I would be driving down the street and I would just say out loud, "I miss Chief." I had many instances like those until I finally learned to

D.Nile Rivers

deal with the break up.

Once I realized that we would be nothing more than friends, I was able to accept his absence from my life a little better. At least I would still have him as a friend even if we couldn't be anything else. We decided to stay in touch. I still loved him very much, but I was willing to do so from a distance. To me, Chief was everything I wanted in a man.

Chapter Ten

Life Goes On

Even though Chief and I resorted to being friends, I still loved him dearly. I kept busy at work to avoid dealing with my feelings of loneliness. I also decided to continue my education and applied to another college in order to get my bachelor's degree in Criminal Justice. But after a while, I got lonely and in my vulnerable state, the devil was able to send a little temptation my way to keep me living in sin. I still wasn't going to church at this point, so it was very easy to keep me lost in my mess. He knew I had a desperate need of wanting to be loved. I kept thinking I could find it in a man, and he was more than willing to feed my thoughts.

I could have easily called Reece, but I hadn't spoken to him since I had met Chief. During the little time I had with Chief, I realized more of what it meant to be loved by someone. Instead of having to do everything and taking the initiative, I was able to experience having someone do for me for a change. I came to realize that I was nothing more than someone Reece used to satisfy his own needs. When I thought about it, I had wasted six years of my life on him for nothing. I wanted to kick myself for all those years I had wasted following him around. Nothing had changed. He still didn't call to speak to Trey who was now four years old. The only reason I stayed in touch with him, from time to time, was because I needed to know that I had a working number to reach him in case I ever needed him.

Nope, I didn't call Reece to get me over my loneliness. I didn't have to call anyone for that matter. Instead, my boss decided to step up his game. He realized that I wasn't seeing anyone and probably saw through the fact that I was in a vulnerable state because he had not given up on trying to get with me. Little by little he started talking to me more and it gave me the opportunity to take my mind off my troubles. I really wasn't interested in him as "my man," but he was nice to talk to and hang out with. He always seemed to be on the go, doing something fun. Before we knew it, we became good friends and talked to each other about our troubles. Along with the talks came the visits to Mom's. He was good. He would come over with baked goods and try to compare cooking tips with Mom. He also came over and shoveled the driveway now and then when it snowed. He was always around at the right moments. He even showed up, unannounced, at certain high school events that I had picked as overtime work driving the bus. It worked out well for him because he was the boss and knew all my assignments. I didn't mind because it provided me with someone to talk to while I waited for the events to end.

The more time I spent with him, the more he grew to like me. I still was not feeling him because he wasn't my type; he was white (I just didn't believe in mixing races at the time). Everyone who knew me knew that I didn't believe in mixing races. So, regardless of how close we got and how much time we spent with each other, I just couldn't do it. This is just where I was during this time in my life.

Eventually, he came to me and told me that he didn't want to be with his girlfriend any more; that they were having issues. As far as I knew, what he told me was true. I didn't consider the fact that he might be lying. I didn't care because I wasn't thinking about him. Regardless of the fact that I wasn't thinking about him, he was thinking about me because he started leaving cards, chocolates, and flowers for me on the windshield of my car. I thought it was nice, but I still wasn't budging. It's not that he was bad looking, either, because he was a handsome man. He had dirty blonde hair, blue eyes, and a nice build. But it just wasn't enough for me to go beyond how I felt about mixing races.

The more he persisted, however, the more I gave in. He knew that I was still trying to get over Chief, but it didn't seem to matter to him. I thought to myself, Chief was out of the picture and the chances of us getting together seemed slim, so I agreed to go out with him. We decided to go shoot pool with a friend of his. I won most of the games and later found out that I won because he let me. But I wasn't a bad pool player. I had spent a lot of my time in Germany shooting pool.

From that one outing with Lenny came many more, and before I knew it, he came to me one day and told me that he and his girlfriend

Finding Mr. Right

had broken up and he was moving out. I questioned him as to whether it had anything to do with me, and he told me that it was something that was in the process of happening prior to meeting me. I believed him. I couldn't really say for certain whether hanging out with me was the icing on the cake or the incentive for him to make it final or whether it was just something that had happened. I would hate to know that it was because of me.

We embarked on a whirlwind romance. If he wasn't buying me flowers, I was buying him flowers. If he wasn't making me dinner (he loved to cook) and trying to impress me, then it was something else. I didn't try to impress him with my cooking because I didn't like to cook to begin with, and I didn't think he would have been too impressed if I had.

I lived in an area that was predominantly White. When we moved into the neighborhood it seemed as if "For Sale" signs sprouted up on lawns everywhere. My family didn't care too much about it because we had just as much of a right to be there as anyone else. I think maybe the neighbors thought we would start having wild parties and playing extremely loud music on a regular basis. Well, they got neither, and eventually just accepted us being there.

When Lenny and I started dating each other, he was made to become aware of the differences in our races and how unacceptable it was for whites and blacks to mix, at least in the area where I lived. It didn't matter if we were sitting in a restaurant or driving down the street together, we got looks. It didn't bother me much because I was used to racial tension and prejudice. He, on the other hand, was not and got defensive from time to time. I did my best to explain to him that I was used to it, but he wasn't used to it, and it really bothered him to the point where he would say something. Not a good idea.

The first time Lenny and I made love was a bit awkward for me. I was a bit hesitant because of old myths I had heard, and simply because it was a first for me. Well, when all was said and done, the experience was a good one. What I realized was that when the lights were off, I couldn't tell what color he was or maybe it was because I had my eyes closed.

What I liked about making love with Lenny was the fact that he was attentive to my needs, and it wasn't a performance like I was used to. Maybe he was trying to impress me, and if that was the case, it worked.

D.Nile Rivers

Approximately two months later, Lenny broke up with me. I was furious. I was beyond mad because I went against what I believed (mixing races) and agreed to give in to his persistent behavior only to have him break up with me. I wasn't giving up without a fight.

He didn't give me a good reason at first, but I knew what it was. Someone had said something to him about his relationship with me and he chickened out. Well, I wasn't having that! Not after all the emotional issues I had dealt with prior to getting involved with him.

I tried to let it go, but I couldn't. He couldn't either. After a while he started seeing me on the down low. His definition of down low meant that he didn't acknowledge that he was seeing me to his friends and family. He still called me, and we still talked, but I spent the majority of the time angry with him for the decision that he had made. The majority of our conversations would end with him pretending to be confused about his feelings and crying over the phone; not a good combination.

One day I decided to surprise him and went to his apartment. He lived in a loft apartment with the parking garage underneath. Based on how the building was made, I was able to see into the garage. I saw that his car was there which meant he was home. When I rang the doorbell, he ignored it. Well, who told him to do that? The more he didn't answer the doorbell, the more I rang it. When he finally answered it, he gave me some story about how he couldn't see me and that it was over between us. I realized that the reason he wouldn't answer the door was because he had a woman in his apartment. I told him that I wasn't leaving until he opened the door. I assured him that I wasn't going to do anything stupid; that I just wanted to talk to him. He finally buzzed me in and hesitantly let me in the apartment. I walked in, and I asked him, "Where is she?"

He said, "Where is who?"

I said, "I know you have someone in here." Sure enough, she was in the bedroom. She was fully dressed. I didn't care so much about her. It was about him. I told her that I didn't have any problems with her, and he told her that she should leave. Once she was out the door, it was on! When he kept lying to me, I picked up his motorcycle helmet and flung it across the room. That got his attention and let him know exactly how upset I was. All I kept asking was, "Why?" That is all the information I needed.

He kept beating around the bush and giving me lame answers and

Finding Mr. Right

excuses. What he didn't understand was that I wasn't leaving until he gave me an explanation as to why he couldn't see me any more, but it was all right for him to see someone else.

I kept accusing him of breaking up with me because I was black. He kept denying it until he finally broke down crying and decided to explain what had caused him to break up with me in the first place. He said that it wasn't acceptable for him to be with me and that his mother had said something to him about being with me. I later found out that this statement was a lie like so many others he would tell. He said that black jokes were made pertaining to me and that he just couldn't deal with it. I looked at him in disgust and with no pity whatsoever. I called him a chicken and any other name I thought of at the time. He kept trying to apologize, but I wasn't hearing it. As a matter of fact, I couldn't hear anything past the anger and rage in my head. I accused him of getting me to fall in love with him and then dumping me without thinking of how I would feel. I left there upset and in disbelief.

This would have been a perfect opportunity for me to let go and spend some time thinking about my life and what I really needed, but I didn't. All I knew was that I had a void that needed to be filled and I kept trying to fill it with a man. Every time I let a man in, I fell for them heart, body and soul, only to have them take that for granted. To me, I felt like I was giving my all and not receiving the same in return. I couldn't understand how I could give so much and receive so little in return. Maybe that was my problem. Maybe I kept giving, thinking they would give back in equal measure. Well, my father always told us, "Treat people the way you want to be treated." I kept thinking that if I treated men the way I wanted to be treated, I would get the same in return. I never did, but I was willing to keep trying until I found one that did. Little did I know that I kept giving them what God wanted me to give Him instead. I hadn't gotten to the part of the Bible in Matthew 22:37 where Jesus said, "Thou shalt love the Lord thy God with all thy heart, and with all thy soul, and with all thy mind." I was so caught up in sin that I couldn't see my way out to save my life. I was exactly where the devil wanted me; on his side.

Chapter Eleven

Caught Up

Lenny and I eventually made up after much harassment on my part. I wasn't about to let go because he had harassed me until I gave in, and he was going to finish what he started. That's how I felt about it.

His family adjusted to his life with a "black woman and child" in it. His father and I got along pretty well, and so did his father's girlfriend and I.

I remember going to his father's house with Trey for dinner one night. We were having dinner and one of his sisters was going to be there. We had never met. When we arrived, we greeted everyone as we walked in and we got nothing in return. His sister didn't speak and neither did her children. I was heated! Lenny didn't walk in with us, so by the time he came in the house I was in the kitchen with his father's girlfriend, Mary, expressing to her how much I didn't appreciate the reception we received. Lenny came into the kitchen and tried to reason with me. After I calmed down, I decided to stay and endure.

That night put things in a whole different perspective for me, but it hadn't changed my mind about being with Lenny.

When I mentioned to my friends that I was seeing a white guy, they couldn't believe it. My girlfriends were full of questions about how he was in bed. My male friends didn't want to hear about that; they were too busy being shocked over the fact that I was with someone outside my race. They knew how adamant I was about staying within my race. When I told Chief about it, he couldn't believe it either. He made his little comments, but as far as I was concerned, he shouldn't have had anything to say other than, "I hope you are happy." I had heard enough about his escapades, since the time we

Finding Mr. Right

broke up, to know that he wasn't any more righteous than I was.

Lenny and I continued to see each other, and he eventually moved in with me to help out financially. He loved my son and they got along well together, but soon after he moved in, I started feeling guilty about living with him. I had never lived with a man before, and I realized this was a big step for Trey and me. For the first time, in the midst of my sinfulness, I actually felt the weight of my sin. Maybe it was just fear. Either way, I had a feeling that God wasn't pleased. If I stopped to think about the lifestyle I had lived up to this point, I would have felt His displeasure with more than just Lenny moving in with me. I would have felt remorse for the life I was living as a whole.

About a month or so after Lenny had moved in, the guilt became overwhelming. I explained my concerns to him about us living together and asked him to move out. He panicked. He thought he was going to lose me. Instead of moving out, he asked me to marry him and I accepted. We had talked about marriage previously, but Lenny hesitated because he didn't want to get married only to have it fail. I tried to reassure him that I wouldn't let him fail, but who would have known.

I agreed to marry Lenny. We talked about it and we both agreed that neither of us would change once we got married. But it didn't work out that way.

The day before we got married, I called my family members and told them about my plans. I left messages for those I couldn't reach. I told them where it was going to be held and that I would be leaving for the honeymoon right after. Well, only two of my friends showed up because nobody else believed me.

I should have known the marriage would be doomed when the Justice of the Peace got lost, we forgot to bring the marriage license, and none of my family members came; I cast any negative thoughts I had aside. We got married and went away for the weekend. When we returned home, our apartment had been robbed, and that was just the beginning.

The first week of marriage came with big warning signs. Lenny decided that he was going to implement some changes even though we had both agreed that we wouldn't. His first change was to tell me that I could no longer have male friends calling the house. I was told to get rid of them altogether. Well, I told him I wasn't going to do that. He was especially concerned about Chief and wanted me to have nothing

D.Nile Rivers

to do with him. I was also supposed to tell Blackie (he and I made up after I finished basic training) that we couldn't be friends any more. Lenny knew that Blackie and I had been friends for ten years. He didn't care. I told him that I wasn't giving up my friends, but that I would tell them not to call the house out of respect for him and to make him feel more at ease.

If it wasn't for the fact that I felt Lenny was making a move to control me, I probably would have been a little more cooperative. But the fact remained that none of the friends he referred to were new. I had already told him about them, so it wasn't as if he wasn't aware. He didn't seem to have a problem before we got married. I found his request to be unreasonable and unwarranted, so I complied in a way that I felt would work. I didn't give up my friends (I had already told him I wouldn't), but I did ask them not to call the house.

The next change came when I was going out one night with the girls, and he proceeded to try to take off the dress I was trying to put on. I thought he had lost his mind. Not only did he keep trying to take the dress off of me, but he also pushed me on the bed. I was in shock. I couldn't believe that he had the audacity to put his hands on me. I told him, "I won't tolerate a black man putting his hands on me, do you really think I'm going to let you put your hands on me?"

Well, he didn't like that too much. I didn't care, so I got dressed and left the house. It got better. Within that same week, he took a picture I had hanging on the wall and broke it over his head during an argument. I immediately picked up the phone and called 911 because I truly thought he had lost his mind. He took the phone from me and hung it up. The police called back to ask if everything was all right. I told them that he was crazy, and they had better come and get him. When the police arrived, I explained to them what had happened, and they asked me what I wanted to do about the situation. I told them that I wanted him out because he couldn't be trusted. They asked me to leave while Lenny got his things together. He left, but I took him back. We talked and tried to work things out by compromising.

I did what I could to make things work, based on where I was mentally and emotionally. I tried becoming a part of his world and he tried to do the same for me. I even took up softball and became the *token* on the softball team (because I could run faster than anyone else), but I didn't really like softball. I was afraid of catching the ball because it was so hard. I preferred batting.

58

Finding Mr. Right

Lenny and I went on hikes with his father and his girlfriend, Mary. We went mountain biking in Vermont with his best friend. We even went to Canada for a weekend to ski. That was a total disaster.

On his part, he tried going out with me to a nightclub one night. The club was predominantly black and Hispanic. Unfortunately, this was the night when all the men I knew decided to go out as well. This wasn't a good thing because Lenny was already insecure as it was. I did what I could to make him feel better by introducing him to my friends, but he just didn't seem comfortable. He tried dancing with me, and as we danced I could see the smirks on my friends' faces. I tried to ignore them. I even had the audacity to ask Lenny if I could dance with one of my friends. Why not? I liked to dance and Lenny didn't want to dance to the majority of the songs. I didn't go out to stand there and bob my head, so I asked him.

I think he got a little angry because by the time the song was over I couldn't find him. I didn't go looking for him either. I just stayed on the dance floor and danced until it was time to go. I thought he would return, but he never did. When I tried to find him as I was leaving the club, he was nowhere to be found. I went to the parking lot where we had parked, but the car was gone. I tried calling him, but I got no response. I ended up having to hitch a ride with someone I had just met.

When I got home I had to climb through the bedroom window to get in the house. Once again, I was heated. According to Lenny, he looked for me but couldn't find me. Yeah, right!

Within a few months, things began to feel a little crowded. As a result, we moved into a two family house. It was a really nice place. It was no longer "my place" but "our place" now, and I think that made a big difference to him. Things were okay for the most part. My only complaint was that he just never seemed to give me the space that I needed. He always seemed to be everywhere I was. It didn't matter if I was using the bathroom, doing my hair, cooking, etc. I realized this was just his thing, but it annoyed the heck out of me.

He also had this annoying habit of checking my skin for blemishes and asking questions about scars on my body. It was always something! I didn't know if he just wanted to know everything about me or if he was truly just curious. Either way, it was a problem for me.

Somewhere along the line we learned to live in harmony. I guess we just learned to deal with and accept each other. I learned not to

59

D.Nile Rivers

play my music when he was around, and he did the same with me. We each had our chores, and there were things he liked to do that I didn't, which worked out well. He liked to cook, and I hated it. I liked to do laundry and keep the house clean, etc.

Lenny taught me how to change the oil and the brakes on my car. He taught me how to work with wood. I was always up for the challenge of learning something new.

Speaking of new, I changed jobs. I became a secretary because Lenny mentioned that he wanted us to have a baby. I told him that I would have a baby for him if he could guarantee a girl.

December of 1995, I got pregnant. Unfortunately at this time, Lenny and I weren't speaking (don't remember why). Words weren't necessary to conceive, so it didn't matter. When I knew I was ovulating, I woke Lenny up and had sex with him. Not very romantic, I know. But it wasn't about romance.

My pregnancy started off well. I thought for sure that I was going to get through this pregnancy without getting sick, but it was worse than my pregnancy with Trey. The doctors did what they could to alleviate my all day sickness and eventually came up with suppositories. It was not fun, but it worked.

Halfway through the pregnancy I was told that my cervix was acting up, and they tried to put me on bed rest. I did what they recommended for a while, but I was so used to being active that it really bothered me to have to be still. Whenever I did try to go out to the grocery store or did much walking it felt like the baby was trying to come out. It wasn't a good feeling so I learned to be still.

Lenny didn't understand the concept of bed rest because he ended up calling me fat and telling me that I was lazy. Comments like these only fueled whatever animosity I already had towards him.

Prior to this point in my pregnancy, Lenny and I had a disagreement that reached the ultimate place of irritation for me. It started off during the day, and he just kept adding fuel to the fire. I warned him that I was getting upset, but he didn't care. I told him that I wouldn't be going to his mother's later on that night for dinner because I didn't want to be there with an attitude. He couldn't drive himself because he had fallen and broken his foot. I agreed to take him, but told him that I wouldn't be staying. He didn't believe me.

When we arrived at his mother's, I went in and said my greetings and told his mother that I was sorry I couldn't stay. As I reached to

Finding Mr. Right

open the door to leave, I heard his mother say, "That bitch." I walked out and fumed as I drove home. I couldn't believe my ears and what made it worse was that she said it in front of my son. When I got home, I called Lenny and asked him if he had heard what his mother had called me. He said that he had and he agreed with her. Well, you make your bed...

I didn't speak to his mother after that day. I told him that unless she apologized she wasn't ever going to see her grandchild. The day I had my daughter Morgan, she called me in the hospital and apologized. I didn't want to accept her apology because I knew the only reason she apologized was so that she could see her granddaughter. I didn't want to accept the apology, but I did.

Lenny was thrilled about his first child and being in the delivery room to watch her being born. I was just glad that it was finally over. I had been miserable and had made people around me miserable. I made sure the doctor did everything necessary to make sure that I would never become pregnant again. I would rather die than go through another pregnancy.

Life as a new mother was tiring initially, but we adjusted. It had been nine years since I had a baby, so I had to learn all over again. It was a special time for me.

Lenny's mom agreed to take care of Morgan during the day while we worked. She lived half an hour away so it was a trek every morning, but it was a blessing to have family take care of the baby as opposed to a stranger.

Because I saw her every day during the week, Lenny's mom and I got to learn more about each other. I even ventured out on a limb and asked her why she hadn't approved of me in the beginning of the relationship and why they had advised Lenny to break up with me. She said that they never told him to break up with me and that it all boiled down to the fact that someone made a joke about black people one day, and Lenny took that and ran with it. I tucked that little bit of information under my hat for another day.

Six months after Morgan was born, I put in to become a police officer at my job. It was something I wanted to do for a long time. Once I got the position, I had to attend a three-month academy. It was difficult for me because Morgan was still so young. I wasn't able to stay at the academy every week like the other recruits. I had to get special permission to drive back and forth every day. My classmates

61

D.Nile Rivers

didn't like this very much, but they didn't understand that I had a baby. They really thought I liked driving back and forth over an hour one way and getting up at four o'clock in the morning to drop Morgan off so that I could report to class on time. It was tough having to do that, but what made it worse was getting home at the end of the day and instead of having peace in the house, I had to deal with Lenny who was jealous of the fact that I was pursuing a dream. Instead of coming home to having dinner made, I had to make it, take care of the baby, help Trey with his homework, and find time for my own sanity. Things got ugly quickly, and I decided that I had enough.

Because of Lenny's insecurities, he thought he could get my attention by putting his hands on me again. That was all it took. I was through with him and it was just a matter of time before we would go our separate ways.

I tried to stick it out, but the stress was just something I didn't need. I had enough to deal with. To make matters even worse, one day Lenny decided to come in to the kitchen while I was sitting with the kids at the table; he took a kitchen knife and said that he was going to kill himself. Well, that was all I needed to form my own conclusions. I thought to myself, "He's crazy enough to think that if he can't have me then no one else can and try to kill the kids and me, before killing himself." So that night I slept with the dresser against the bedroom door. When I got to the academy the following morning, I asked for permission to come in late the next day because I needed to go to court to file for a restraining order against psycho.

I filed the restraining order, and later that evening the Sheriff's department served him. He was told to leave and to keep his distance. He was crushed, but I felt it was necessary.

Morgan's first birthday was just around the corner. He threw a birthday party for her at my house, and it was around this same time that I told Morgan's godmother (whom I was renting from) that I was looking for a more affordable place to live. I told her that I had filed for a separation from Lenny.

Up to this point she hadn't believed the stories I had told her about what I was dealing with in my marriage, but during the party, Lenny flipped a switch or something and went off on her and my other girlfriend. That was all she wrote. They thought he was crazy and apologized for not believing me sooner.

Finding Mr. Right

Chapter Twelve

Blast from the Past

Once I filed for legal separation from Lenny, all bets were off. I wasn't divorced, but I wasn't dead either. I spoke to various members of my family in regards to getting a divorce and it was frowned upon. Ultimately, I knew the decision would be mine. Even though I had explained to them about the controlling and occasional physical abuse, they didn't seem to think that I had a problem. I was even told to get over it. With this kind of advice and lack of concern, I decided to make my own decision.

I knew that I wanted a divorce, but I was afraid that he would meet me on the steps of the courthouse with a gun and try to kill me. It wasn't unheard of, and I just didn't know where his head was. I decided that I would wait. There really wasn't a rush to get the divorce because I wasn't interested in getting married again. I figured that I would just wait it out until he had gotten over the fact that we weren't going to be together.

The separation was hard at first because we shared custody of Morgan. I had given him this gift of having a child, and I didn't want to take that away from him. The only problem with sharing custody meant that I had to see him and deal with him. Dealing with him meant that I had to listen to him try to appeal to my good side (didn't have one at the time) and try to work things out.

I eventually gave in because I couldn't deal with not having Morgan all the time. But no sooner had he moved in than he started searching my things and asking about guys, etc. On one occasion, Mom came to visit and Lenny verbally disrespected her out of frustration. As a result, I told him to leave. He didn't want to hear it, but that was the only option he had. I knew then that I wasn't going to

63

D.Nile Rivers

deal with his insecurities again. I didn't want Trey and Morgan growing up and thinking our relationship was the norm either.

Once he was gone, life went on as usual and I purposed in my mind that I was going to take the next year to get myself together. I wanted to take time to figure out what went wrong and do some self-evaluating.

Things started out that way, but to get past the loneliness and to avoid going into a depressive state, I started going out and meeting guys. In other words, I did what I knew worked for me. But I was cold towards them. I was angry because my marriage didn't last. I was angry because I trusted that Lenny loved me enough to live up to my expectations; what I needed in a man. In my mind, he had let me down. I didn't stop to think that maybe I had let myself down by expecting him to be something he couldn't be. I was still trying to fill a void within me, but I kept getting the same results: disappointed.

I wasn't ready or in the mood to deal with men on a relationship level. I just wanted something to take my mind off my disappointment. They didn't care though and tried whatever they could. Some couldn't believe that I truly wasn't interested in them. Nothing had changed; men were still men and the games were still being played. The only difference now was that I was playing it too, but even that got boring.

One day, out of the blue, I decided to call Chief. I hadn't seen him in about five years. We had kept in touch from time to time, but that was all. I told him that I was separated from Lenny and that I wanted to take a trip out to see him and catch up. Well, who told me to do that? I drove three hours to New Jersey to see him.

Chief agreed to meet me at a gas station that was located off the highway near his house because I didn't know where I was going. I got there early. I was so nervous. I didn't know if I would even recognize him. When he drove up, I thought he would just motion to me to follow him, but he got out of the car to get a hug. He looked so good! He hadn't changed at all, and when he hugged me, that hadn't changed either. I was taken back by the chemistry and the emotions that resurfaced from a single hug. I tried to pretend as if it meant nothing, but I knew he felt it too. We had that "thing" between us. He gave me the once over look and smiled in appreciation. It was all good. We tore ourselves away from each other so that we could get back in our cars and get to our destination.

We ended up going to dinner. We talked and ate and stared at each

64

Finding Mr. Right

other the entire time. It was as if we were taking as many notes as possible and trying to commit them to memory so that we had something to look back on. We got caught up on what had occurred throughout the years and he informed me that he had recently broken up with his girlfriend. I couldn't even pretend to feel sorry because that just meant opportunity for me.

Before we knew it, time had gone by way too quickly, and it was time for me to leave. I had a three-hour drive back home, and I had someone watching the kids. I didn't want to leave and he didn't want me to leave either. I promised him that I would be back to visit. He hugged me before I left and kissed me like only he could, and sent me on my way.

I had a lot to think about on my way home that night. I tried replaying everything that was said at dinner. I tried remembering everything about his face, his smile, and his eyes. His eyes were brown, but they weren't the average brown. They weren't hazel, but they weren't dark brown either. They were close to resembling caramel and mocha mixed together. Whatever the color, they had a tendency to hypnotize me and make me feel like I was the only person in his world when he looked at me. Yes ladies, it was like that!

I got lost going home because I was caught up reminiscing about the past and what could be. Once I realize that I had veered off track, I pulled over to the side of the road, pulled out my atlas, and regrouped. Being in the military had its perks.

I couldn't help thinking about him. As a matter of fact, I purposely kept thinking about him. I even called him to tell him how I was feeling, and he confessed to having similar feelings.

When I finally got home I had already made up my mind that I was going to see him and soon. He was single, and I was separated, unattached as far as I was concerned. I was determined to make an effort to pick up where we left off so many years before.

I went to see him as often as I could, and things between us got hot and heavy quickly. He always seemed eager to greet me and happy to see me when I arrived. The sex was good as usual, but this time I wanted more. I wanted to be his. I had heard about all his flings during the past five years, and I had entertained all his stories without so much as letting him know how each fling was like a knife in my heart. I had never stopped loving him. I had to let him go back then because I didn't stand a chance against what he was going through at the time.

65

D.Nile Rivers

But it was not to be.

I went to see him one night and during one of our conversations he mentioned that he wished we could be together, but that in order for me to be the perfect woman for him, he would have to take bits and pieces from other women to make me into his perfect woman. I was devastated when I heard this, but I didn't let it show. I knew then that I would never be enough for him. I made up my mind that I would just take what I could get as long as it meant that I would be with him.

On one particular morning as I was heading home from seeing him, he called me and asked me if I had seen anyone sitting on the stairs outside his building when I left. I told him that I hadn't seen anyone. He told me that his previous girlfriend, the one he had broken up with recently, had met him on the stairs as he was leaving for work. I told him that I hadn't seen her. I asked him, "What did she want?"

He said, "She doesn't want us to be over."

I didn't say much about it. I just let it go.

The last week of December, a couple months into us seeing each other, I got a call from Chief. I hadn't heard from him in almost a month. I had stopped calling him because I wanted him to take the initiative. I wanted him to be about me for a change. He hadn't driven three hours to see me, and I just wanted more. I wanted him to show me that he was serious about us getting together. He was a bit quiet on the phone. I didn't say much. He's not the type of person to call and be quiet, so I realized that something was up. I wasn't prepared for what he said next. He said, "Kellis is pregnant".

I said, "What? How could Kellis be pregnant when we are seeing each other?" My heart broke even further. It had already been broken when I stopped seeing him years before, but now it was worse.

He said, "You live so far away, and she just kept coming around." He said, "I didn't mean for it to happen."

I asked him, "So what are you going to do?"

He said, "I can't ask her to get rid of it. So I'm going to do the right thing and marry her."

Wow! I couldn't believe my ears. There really wasn't much I could say. Then he said, "But I still want to see you on the side."

Once again I was to be the "other woman." I didn't think so. I calmly told him, "I love you, and I want to be with you, but I won't be the other woman." I got off the phone and I tried to drown myself in my tears. I had the strange feeling of being numb yet able to feel at the

Finding Mr. Right

same time. How is that possible?

I got duped or, rather, I got played. I knew it was difficult for him to call me and confess to the fact that he was seeing us both at the same time, but I knew it was even harder for him to have to tell me that she was pregnant. In a way he did me a favor. For all I knew, he could have continued to see us both without either one of us knowing. His first mistake was two-timing me, and the second was not using a condom. I was so angry with him, but I didn't let him know. I simply took the news and swallowed it.

I didn't speak to him for a long time after that. When I spoke to him again, he had gotten married and had a new baby girl. I asked about his other children and married life. He was miserable! I was glad, but I didn't show it. It served him right! I wasn't sorry for him in the least. I was just angry that he could be so stupid.

Even though I knew I was better off without him, I didn't love him any less. But I knew I had to let him go because he was no longer available. Once again it was hard to do, but I did it.

Chapter Thirteen

Next Best Thing

Letting go of Chief was becoming a habit, and like the last time, I dealt with it by keeping busy. As much as I wanted to sink into the abyss of depression, I couldn't. I had two kids depending on me.

I was now a police officer at the local college in the town where I lived and I was also a reserve police officer in my town. I had a lot going on. I was a domestic violence investigator, a rape investigator, and a bike patrol and community police officer. I enjoyed talking to the students and mingling with the faculty and staff on campus. I also liked the freedom of being able to walk around instead of sitting at a desk all day. I still had a few classes to complete in order to get my degree, but I was almost there.

Based on all I was doing, I didn't have the time to get involve in another relationship like I normally did. I had guys that I spoke to on a fairly regular basis, but that was all we did.

February 1999, about fourteen months after I gave up on ever reconciling with Lenny, I met Manny. We met each other at Gym Night Madness (an all night gym party) years before, but I was too busy strung out on Chief at the time to pay him any attention. It didn't matter to me how attractive he was, I didn't believe in being involved with more than one person at the same time. I didn't have the ability to focus my emotions on more than one man at the same time. It just wasn't something I liked to do.

I got involved with a group of disc jockeys who started a "Soul Café" forum for local talent. I had been around disc jockeys since I was seventeen, so I was familiar with a lot of them. My role was to schedule the performances and take the information of the participants. During one particular meeting for the Soul Café, I started talking to

Finding Mr. Right

one of the DJs, Jay, from out of town. He was easy on the eyes, but I wasn't interested in having a relationship with him. I decided that he would just be in my life for conversation purposes.

Jay tried to run a game on me, which was evident to me, but I let him talk because he humored me. We struck up a friendship from that day and talked often. It was usually about him wanting to be with me. It was never actually said, but implied in many other ways.

On one particular night of the Soul Café, Jay and I agreed to meet at the club and hang out with each other. When I got there, he hadn't arrived yet so I mingled with the other members of the group.

As I was talking to the head of the group, I noticed a man walk through the door of the club. It was almost like the day I met Chief when he had walked down the hall. I checked him out as he walked towards where we were standing. I asked Mike, the head of the group, "What's that guy's name, again?"

"Who, Manny?"

"Yeah, that's it." Manny walked towards us smiling. The way he walked spoke of his self-confidence. He wore a tan sweater pulled tightly across the width of his chest. His shoulder-length locks were pulled back in a ponytail, and he was just as smooth as could be. He said, "Hello, goodnight."

I returned the greeting and flirted saying, "Long time no see."

He acknowledged my flirting, and we struck up a small conversation about nothing much until we parted ways.

For the rest of the night I was like a bee drawn to honey – again! I kept my eyes on him all night. I made sure I knew where he was at all times. In the meantime, I looked out for Jay. He hadn't arrived yet and I hoped he wouldn't because that would totally mess up my play for Manny.

Manny had his brother with him. We were introduced and we decided to play a game of pool until the activities began. Manny hung out nearby, but didn't play. Instead, his brother decided to flirt with me, but I wasn't interested. I only entertained him enough to keep the chatter going during the game.

As we played, I noticed Jay had arrived and was standing by watching us. I was disappointed that he came, but I was determined to work around that. I was still in the middle of the game and chatting back and for with Manny's brother while Jay watched, but the entire time I was planning in my mind how I could talk to Manny without

69

D.Nile Rivers

making it obvious that I was totally trying to ignore Jay in the process.

When the game was finally over, Jay and I hung out for a little bit as the crowd started to arrive. As we talked, I was pre-occupied with my thoughts of Manny. I did everything I could to maintain my interest in the conversation with Jay, while maintaining a focus on Manny. I noticed everything Manny did, who he spoke to, and where he went the entire time I was with Jay. Later, when I saw a female talking to Manny at the bar, I felt my jealousy rear its ugly head. I was a little surprised, especially since I had just met him and there was nothing going on between us yet.

As I kept my focus on Manny and talked to Jay at the same time, I saw Manny walking towards us. He came up behind Jay and handed me a drink and walked away. Now, I hadn't asked him for a drink, and he didn't know what I liked to drink, but I accepted it anyway and took that as a sign that he was digging me as much as I was digging him. Jay didn't say anything, but I knew he didn't miss what had transpired.

The club started filling up and the activities began. Artist after artist performed their poetry and sang their songs. Me, I was doing everything and anything I could to lose Jay and hang out with Manny.

Since we were all part of the group putting on the event, we all hung out together near the DJ's booth. Among us were people I knew from the music industry as well as people I had worked with previously in another arena. One person in particular was a female singer, Cassy. I knew her because I was an extra in her first music video. I knew she had a boyfriend, so I wasn't too concerned with her until I saw her flirting with Manny. He played right along, knowing I was paying attention.

Manny and I struck up little conversations here and there throughout the night, while Jay mingled with other members of the group. Whenever I spoke to Manny, I made sure I knew where Jay was at the same time.

Manny and I took the infrequent moments we had to find out little things about each other. Whenever I wasn't talking to him, Cassy was doing whatever she could to corner his attention. Manny enjoyed every bit of the attention he was getting between the two of us. I could tell because as I watched him with her, it was clear that he was flirting right back. He even took his dreads out of the ponytail and shook them free as an attempt to upgrade his sexy. I later learned that this was Something he did when he wanted to appear even sexier than he

70

Finding Mr. Right

already was.

Manny was not the type of guy that you would look at and say, "He is so fine." He was more the type of guy you would look at and do a double take because it was just something about him that drew you to him. He stood about five feet and eight inches tall. He had a broad back with a broad chest to match. He had a flat stomach, a must in my book, and he dressed classy with a touch of sexy on the side. His eyes looked dreamy, as if he was sleepy all the time, and he had shoulder length dreads. You could tell that he lifted weights because he had big arms. In one word, Manny was "handsome." He had a physique that reminded me of Chief.

When Manny took out his ponytail, I knew exactly what effect he was going for, and I smiled. I didn't like the fact that Cassy was falling for this ploy, but I think he was doing it for my benefit. Even when I wasn't talking to him or trying not to look at him, he knew. He was playing a game, and I was playing right along.

Plans were made to hang out after the Café was over. I could hear Jay and Mike talking about it. Jay asked me if I was going to go with them and I told him that I was ready to hit the road. I knew that Manny and his brother were leaving, and I hadn't gotten to spend as much time with him as I had wanted to. I realized that I had to do something because if he left I wouldn't know how to get in touch with him. The problem I had was trying to get his number without Jay seeing and being aware that I was interested in Manny. I'm sure he already realized this to some degree, but hadn't said anything all night. Jay and I weren't in a relationship, but I knew that he liked me, and I didn't want to hurt his feelings.

When I saw Manny walking towards the exit, I told Jay that I was leaving. Jay decided to walk me to my car and ended up getting in the car. Of course I knew where Manny was the entire time. He had already gotten in his brother's car, which was parked on the street corner. I was parked a little ways down the street. When Jay got in my car he decided that he wanted to have a conversation. Well, I wasn't in the mood for a conversation because I was trying to catch up to Manny.

I did what I could to reassure Jay and told him that I would call him. I dropped him near the entrance gate of the club and drove off. As I got to the corner, Manny and his brother were pulling away. I flashed my headlights and blew my horn until they pulled over. Once they did, Manny's brother came out of the car and approached my

D.Nile Rivers

window. I told him that I was wondering if Manny wanted to ride back with me. He went back to his car and Manny got out. I unlocked the passenger side door, and he got in. I was all smiles, and Manny was all about being nonchalant and smooth.

During the ride back we talked and learned more about each other. I made sure and told Manny that I was tired of playing games, and that I was all about honesty. He told me that he wasn't seeing anyone and gave me his number. When we got to his destination, he gave me his phone number and told me to call him. He kissed me on the cheek and got out of the car. What a night!

The next day, I did everything I could to prevent myself from calling him. By the evening time, I just couldn't take it any more, and I called him. I was surprised to find that it was the right number. Usually, guys gave you a beeper number, but not their home number. I figured the only time they give you a home number is if they didn't live with anyone, or if they are legit. I had a lot to learn. This was a whole different game for me.

Manny and I got close very quickly, but before you knew it, I was frustrated and ready to call it quits. I wasn't used to being in a relationship with someone like Manny. He just never seemed to have time for me. Every time we set aside time to be together, someone would call or need him for something, and he would just go. I never understood that.

A few months into the relationship, Blackie came to me and asked me if I knew about Manny's background. I didn't know what he was talking about. I thought maybe history was about to repeat itself and he was going to tell me that Manny was married. Instead he said, "Manny has a criminal record."

I looked at him and said, "What are you talking about?"

He said, "Don't you know who he is?" I looked at him bewildered and at the same time tried to prepare myself for the worst. He told me that Manny had a record and that I should ask him about it. I didn't ask Manny, but not too long after Blackie told me this news, a female friend, an old high school classmate, also asked me about my knowledge of Manny's background. At this point, I thought to myself, "Why is it that everyone is trying to tell me about Manny's background?" I didn't admit to knowing anything because I wanted to hear what she had to say. She told me that he had a criminal record and that it had been all over the news when it happened. I simply told

72

Finding Mr. Right

her, "Manny's past is the past, and I am judging him based on who he is now." I wanted to give Manny the benefit of the doubt, to think that he had changed from the person they knew into the man I had grown to love.

Later on that day, I decided to ask Manny about his record which he had so conveniently forgotten to share with me. He told me how he obtained his record and explained that he was innocent. He said that because he refused to give up the individual involved, he took the rap and went to jail. As he spoke, I could see the pain and the anger he still had from the experience. Someone close to him had betrayed him, and even though it had been years, he was still hurting. I thanked him and did what I could to reassure him that I loved him for who he was now and that I wasn't going to change.

With that out of the way, we went on with the relationship. I became more aware of why people felt the need to explain Manny's past to me. They thought it would be a conflict of interests because I was a police officer and he was a felon. I took all that into consideration and still decided to stick it out with Manny. I was relieved that he wasn't married and that I wasn't the other woman – again. But I had no idea. What goes around comes around.

Manny and I had our ups and downs. My main complaint dealt with the issue of spending time together. I tried breaking up with him on more than one occasion because I felt that I needed more. I told him in the beginning of the relationship that I wasn't going to try to change who he was. I told him that I would try to deal with him, but if there came a time when I couldn't, that I would leave. But Manny wouldn't allow me to break up with him; every time I tried, he did whatever it took to please me, and when I was nice and happy, he went right back to being himself.

Once, I broke up with him for about a month. He called me all the time trying to work things out. Even his sister called me to ask me to take him back because he seemed so miserable. I loved Manny and I didn't want him to be miserable, but I just couldn't deal with feeling insignificant and unimportant. It just seemed that regardless of what we had going on, all it took was a phone call, and he would leave. This just kept reaffirming to me that I wasn't important.

One day we took a trip to Niagara Falls. It was a beautiful place to be, but it was a place for people who were in love. I tried holding Manny's hand while we were there walking together, but he wasn't

D.Nile Rivers

mentally with me; he seemed very distant. I took all this in and pulled back on my affections and did what I could to enjoy the scenery. It was hurtful, but it was reality.

While we were there we had plans to go over to the Canadian side of the border. When we crossed the border, Manny got a phone call from his son's mother. I don't know what she said to him other than he needed to come back and deal with his son. There was nothing I could do. I was upset! I couldn't believe he would end our trip and drive back six hours because his son was acting up! Instead of telling her that we were out of town, and he would deal with the issue when he got back, he simply said, "Okay." I didn't know then, but there was more to Manny's life than I knew.

On another occasion, Manny and I went to Maryland to visit some friends he grew up with. I felt important knowing that he thought enough of me to want to introduce me to some of his life long friends. I had already met all his family members, who always had something to say about how skinny they thought I was. But this was in addition to meeting them, and it meant we were getting away from our part of the world and seeing something different together.

It was a good trip down. When we got there I was introduced to everyone and I was made to feel like family. It was a good feeling.

Unfortunately, something happened while we were there to ruin everything. The second day we were there, we went to a store to pick up some items for his friends. I stayed in the car while Manny went in to get what was needed. While he was in the store, his cell phone rang, and I answered it. Who told me to do that? A woman on the other end of the phone asked for Manny. I told her that he was not able to come to the phone at the moment. She then asked, "Who are you?"

I asked, "Who are you?"

I told her that I was Manny's girlfriend. She was shocked. I told her that I would let him know that she called. Well, when Mr. Manny came back to the car, I was fit to be tied! I told him that one of his girlfriends had called while he was in the store. He looked at me as if he didn't know what I was talking about.

I asked him who she was, and he said, "Oh, she is that psycho ex-girlfriend I told you about."

"Then why is she calling you?"

"Because she's crazy."

I just couldn't understand. I was confused as to why an ex-

Finding Mr. Right

girlfriend, who he claimed was psycho, was calling him, especially if he didn't want to have anything to do with her. As he continued to try to explain himself away, I decided to get out of the car while we were stopped at a red light. I had heard enough, and I could feel the rage building inside of me. I needed to walk it off. I got out of the car in the middle of traffic and safely made it to the sidewalk.

I decided to take a walk through the neighborhood. I didn't know where I was, but at that moment it was safer for me to be away from Manny, or I might have done something I would have regretted later.

When he got a chance, Manny found his way down the street where I was. He parked the car and leaned against it while he waited for me to calm down. Somehow he had realized that I needed some space, and it wouldn't be wise to approach me.

I spent the time trying to calm down. When I was able to speak, I returned to the car and listened to what he had to say. All I said to him was, "I don't want you speaking to her any more." Aside from that, I said nothing.

I tried not to let the phone call ruin my time in Maryland. I got past my anger and did what I could to get back in the swing of things. Manny was on his best behavior and willing to do anything to get back in my good graces. His plan worked, and once again I was back to being the loving girlfriend.

But that wouldn't be the last time I would speak with other women on the phone. Women just always seemed to be calling Manny, but I trusted him. Ever since the Maryland incident, I believed him when he assured me that there was nothing going on outside our relationship.

Manny lived alone on the third floor of a three-family house. I tried spending time there, but his phone rang all hours of the night into the early morning. I rarely answered it, but he told me that he had nothing to hide, and if I wanted to answer the phone I could. When I did answer the phone, on more than one occasion, it was usually a woman. I was always polite and took messages. I trusted Manny and had no fear that he would cheat on me. But because of the constant ringing of the phone, I told him that I couldn't sleep at his house anymore because I needed my rest. He didn't mind.

In an attempt to do more things together, we decided to go out dancing to one of the clubs that I liked to visit. I got upset with him that night because he took off, and I couldn't find him. He danced one dance with me and said that he didn't like to dance to every song. I, on

75

D.Nile Rivers

the other hand, could dance all night. It was customary for me to go out to the club and spend the entire night on the dance floor until I was ready to leave. It wasn't my thing to go to the club and stand around, drink, or meet men. I was there only to dance.

On this particular night, I wanted to spend my night dancing with Manny. Unfortunately for me, he didn't have the same intentions. I was disappointed. He told me that I could dance without him, and he would just watch. I told him that I danced by myself all the time, and if that's what I wanted to do I wouldn't have brought him along with me. We got into a disagreement and left. We agreed not to go out dancing with each other again to avoid future disappointments.

We didn't stick to that agreement, though. The next time we tried to go to the club, we decided that I would dance by myself, and if he heard a song that he liked, he would come and dance with me. Well, in the midst of my dancing and having a good time, Manny decided to take a hike, and I couldn't find him. I walked the club over and over again, but he was nowhere to be found. Eventually, I gave up and went to the car to wait for him. When I got there, he was at the car. He said, "I was waiting for you." Once again, I was heated!

If it wasn't one thing, it was another. Manny had a hard time finding a job because of his record. This only added to his anger of having been punished for a crime he didn't commit. He finally got a job with a car rental company in Connecticut where his sister worked. He said that he did repairs on the rental cars and also had an additional duty to go after cars that hadn't been returned on time. At least this is what he told me. So there were times when he called me and told me that he couldn't see me because he would be out until the wee hours of the morning trying to get vehicles. I believed him. Whatever he told me was regarded as the truth. I didn't have any reason not to trust him.

Finding Mr. Right

Chapter Fourteen

Change of Plans

One year into our relationship, while lying in bed with Manny, I clearly heard these words, "You are nothing without God." I had recently heard these same words on two other occasions from two different people that I knew. When I heard it this time I knew God was trying to get my attention. I didn't say anything to Manny right away. I needed to have a talk with God first.

By the end of that day, I was ready to get down on my knees and ask God to forgive me of my sins and to change my life. I had a lot to repent about.

I cried, as I emptied out my heart to God, ashamed of all I had done. By the time I got off my knees, I felt like a load had been lifted off of me, and I was set free. Free from a life that had been bound by sin.

I knew that I had to tell Manny about the change in me, but I wasn't sure he would understand when I told him that there were certain things I couldn't do anymore. When I told him that we couldn't have sex anymore, even though I knew we had been having it all along, and that I wouldn't be going to the clubs any more either, he was very supportive. He said that he respected my decision. I knew it was going to be hard because we were very much into sex; remember, it was like a drug to me.

Besides Manny, I had to let my acquaintances and friends know about the change in my life. Not everybody understood, but for the most part they respected the decision I had made. One of my females friends, Trina, whom I hung out with, drank with, etc., clearly didn't Understand and told me that I should only follow some of the rules in

77

the Bible.

She said, "How can you expect Manny to stop having sex with you, and you guys have been doing it for a year?" She said, "Why can't you just follow *some* of the rules in the Bible?"

I tried to explain to her that I couldn't pick and choose what commandments I should follow and that it just didn't work that way. I also explained to her that Manny respected my decision and was willing to wait until we got married.

Three years later, March 5, 2002, Manny and I got married. The sad part of this day was that he and I weren't even speaking. We got into a disagreement that morning, I don't remember about what, but we were still willing to go through with the decision we had made. We decided to get married by the Justice of the Peace (JOP) for now and then have a big wedding where we would invite our friends and family later that June. We met up with each other in a parking lot near where we were to be wed. The JOP picked us up in her car and took us to her house. When the ceremony was finished, Manny and I were on our way to speaking again.

When we got in the JOP's car for the ride back to our cars, Manny said, "I don't feel any different." I rolled my eyes. I didn't know what he expected it to feel like.

Married life with Manny was different from my first marriage. Instead of Manny wanting to be a part of the family and doing things together, he would say to me, "We have a lifetime together." He took his time about doing things; moving into where I lived as we had agreed, and moving out of his place. Aside from the fact that we were married, not too much had changed. He was still Manny.

He had a lack of enthusiasm, which frustrated me. I had problems dealing with his silent treatment, as well. He had periods of time when he would just "go into his cave" and act like I wasn't there. There were also instances when he would make plans to go away and hang out with his friends and not find it necessary to talk to me about it. He would just walk out of the house as if I wasn't there.

I tried to explain to him about certain things involved in marriage. I wasn't an expert, but I was always reading and trying to better myself in order to be a better wife. This was my second marriage, and I wanted it to work. Whenever I brought up his behavior, he would always say, "I've never been married before, so I don't know."

Two months after we got married, I got a phone call from Psycho,

Finding Mr. Right

Manny's ex-girlfriend. Imagine my surprise. She was not happy. She was hurt and shocked that Manny and I had gotten married, and she wanted an explanation. What was shocking to me was that she had my number and knew that we had gotten married. Not only did she know that, but she also knew everything about our lives up to the day. I smiled and did what I could to pretend that I wasn't dying inside. I let her talk. She told me that she had never broken up with Manny and that they had been together the entire three years that he and I had been together. What goes around comes around. Who knew? She also explained to me that she had confronted him and told him that she was going to call me and tell me everything.

Well, I couldn't wait for Manny to come home that night. I prayed about it, I cried about it, and I really didn't know what I was going to do or say about it except that I wanted an explanation. I needed to know why he did this to me.

I promised Psycho that I would get back in touch with her and that we would confront him together by the end of the week. I tried to keep that promise, but I knew there was no way I was going to be able to keep what I knew quiet for that long. Subsequently, I called her back and we made a plan. We agreed to meet at Manny's job that evening to confront him. I told her that I would call him and tell him that I would bring him dinner as an excuse for showing up at his job. Meanwhile, she and I planned to meet at the top of the street where he worked so that we could figure out the details.

When we met each other, we were both amazingly calm. I told her that I would go meet Manny and once I got him in the car with me, I would call her preprogrammed number in my phone, and she could pull up beside my car.

Once I got Manny in the car, he couldn't stop talking. He told me that he had been trying to get in touch with me all day to tell me that Psycho had called him and was going to harm me.

I looked at him and said, "Harm me? I'm a cop. I have a gun." Then I asked him, "Why is Psycho calling you anyway? I thought you didn't speak to her any more?"

He had some mumble jumble excuse. When he was finished mumbling, I told him that Psycho had called me earlier in the day. I had secretly called her already, and as she pulled up alongside my car, Manny's face froze. It was priceless! She got out of her car and came by my window. We pretended as if we had never met and she

79

D.Nile Rivers

introduced herself to me. I looked at him and asked, "How does she know where you work if you don't have anything to do with her?"

If looks could kill, that girl would have been dead. I calmly said to him, "How could you do this to her? And how could you do this to me?" That was all I wanted to know.

He had nothing to say. Psycho gave me her number and told me to call her if I had any questions I needed answered. She said a few choice words to Manny and left. Manny's eyes followed her as she got in her car and drove away. We sat in silence for a while. There was really nothing further to say. After a few moments, he got out of the car, and I drove home in tears.

I didn't know what I was going to do. I had already sent out half of the invitations for the June wedding, and I had spent so much money on preparations. Mom was already sewing my wedding dress, the tuxedos were already rented, and half the invitations had already been mailed. I wanted to call it off, but it wouldn't really matter because we were already married. Many people didn't know it, but those close to us did. Instead, I prayed and I fasted for an entire week, asking God, "Why?"

By the end of the week, what was revealed to me was this: I had placed Manny above God in my heart. I had placed him on a pedestal as the perfect man with the expectation that he would be perfect in every way. I knew there was no such thing as a "perfect person," but to me, I perceived him as the perfect man for me—someone who loved me and would never hurt me.

I was reminded that no one is perfect, not even Manny. I was told that because he wasn't perfect, he would make mistakes and that my expectations of him were unreasonable. I was shown how I had placed my trust in Manny instead of God, and that I shouldn't have because God is the only one who would never fail me. I was also reminded of my years with Reece and how we had a relationship behind his wife's back. What goes around comes around.

"But he that doeth wrong shall receive for the wrong which he hath done: and there is no respect of persons."
(Colossians 3:25)

Once I accepted this revelation, I was able to forgive Manny, realizing that God had forgiven me when I had done the same thing,

Finding Mr. Right

and if God could forgive me, who was I not to forgive?

"Forbearing one another, and forgiving one another, if any
man have a quarrel against any: even as Christ forgave you,
so also do ye." (Colossians 3:13)

I realized that Manny was only human and I understood that my expectations of him were unrealistic. But even though I forgave him, there came a moment when my flesh took over and I charged at him in rage. Manny hadn't apologized and his smugness got the best of me. Thank God it was just a moment.

Not too long after this incident, Manny started going to church and ultimately accepted Christ into his life.

Within a short period of time after Manny got saved, he got sick and was in bed for a week with flu-like symptoms. The devil was obviously not pleased with his decision. I wasn't able to stay home and take care of him because I had military obligations. I felt relieved knowing that Mom would be there to tend to his needs until I returned.

I kept in touch with Manny while I was away for my two-week military assignment. I also kept in touch with Mom for updates. Mom had spent the majority of her life as a nurse so I trusted her judgment.

When I returned from my duty, I asked Manny to make an appointment with his doctor. After I pestered him about it, he went and came back telling me that they didn't find anything wrong. By this time, Manny had lost approximately twenty pounds within a four-week period. I knew something was wrong.

I made arrangements for him to see a different doctor because I didn't trust the opinion of his doctor who hadn't done any extensive tests to see if there really was a problem. According to his doctor, he was the right weight for his body type.

Something was seriously wrong, but instead of Manny being concerned, he kept looking in the mirror and admiring his lack of body fat. He thought he looked good, but he was extremely thin. His clothes didn't fit him anymore, and I just knew something was wrong.

When he went to the new doctor, they ordered all kinds of lab work and ran tests, but the results were going to take a while to come back.

The wedding day came, and I spent the morning of my wedding day in tears while I put the finishing touches on the hall. I was hurting

D.Nile Rivers

because I had waited for this day for three years and it wasn't anything like I had imagined. So much had happened, and it was weighing heavily on me. Besides that, Manny and I got into an argument that morning, and he left the house upset. Not again!

I did what I could to get past the disagreement and decided that I would make the best of my wedding day. It was all right that Manny wasn't in the house because I didn't want him to see me before the actual ceremony anyway.

The ceremony was to be held at Stanley Park, which was not far from our house. I had made arrangements to have the ceremony in the rose garden by the waterfall. It was beautiful. Unfortunately, Mom, my two sisters, and the minister (my brother-in-law) got lost on their way to the park. I didn't realize this until I had already walked down the walkway and stood next to Manny. Where was the minister? I looked around at my confused guests and made light of the situation. Time was getting short and someone mentioned to me that we had to hurry up because another wedding was scheduled after ours.

Seeing that we were already officially married, I asked my brother, the only family there at the time besides Trey and Morgan, if he would simply pray over us and bless our union. By the time he had finished praying, my lost siblings and Mom had arrived just in time to take pictures.

Things were moving so swiftly, due to lack of time, that I didn't notice the disappointment on the faces of the late arrivals. I tried to explain why we didn't wait for them. I had so much going on and so many people trying to get my attention that I think my apology got lost in the chaos.

By the time we got to the reception, Manny and I had on our game faces on. Things hadn't been fully straightened out regarding the disagreement earlier that day. He did take the time to apologize while we were taking pictures. I accepted his apology, but I couldn't shake my mood.

When we entered the reception hall no one suspected that things weren't great between us, but when my two closest friends found me in the coat closet moping, they realized that something was wrong. I told them that Manny and I had a disagreement earlier. They knew I was not the type of person who was able to mask what I felt. I wanted to, but I couldn't. They offered to get me a bottle of wine, which I gratefully accepted.

Finding Mr. Right

I made the best of the day by socializing with everyone. I tried to sit down, but I was too busy trying to make sure that everything went smoothly. I barely had a chance to spend time with Manny. I tried not to let it bother me. I decided to overcome my impending state of depression by spending as much time with the guests as possible.

The only time I got to spend time with Manny was the first dance. It started off awkward. There was still tension between us, but as the music played ("Spend my Life with "You," by Eric Benet and Tamia), I relaxed as I listened to the words of the song that had become very meaningful to me. Once the dance was over, we were back to socializing until it was time to cut the cake. We made it through that as well, long enough to please our guests and maintain the charade.

From what I gathered, the day turned out swell. Whatever issues arose were taken care of by my family members who turned out to be my strength that day. By the time it was over, I was so exhausted that I just went to sleep.

Our lives continued as usual after the wedding. I resigned as a police officer and became a secretary on campus. I needed a change. Manny got more involved in church, and it was noticeable to his friends, family, co-workers and me, that he was serious about the decision he had made to serve God. He even decided to get baptized along with me at the next baptism ceremony in a few months.

But even with all this, things between Manny and I were up and down. He still couldn't maintain any weight. We still hadn't gotten the test results back. Manny wasn't concerned about his health. I kept commenting on his weight, but that only made him hide from me whenever he took his clothes off. Maybe my constant comments about something being wrong bothered him, but Manny didn't talk much. All I knew was that he was withdrawn and I spent the majority of my time frustrated and trying not to get angry.

Manny and I were still having our issues by the time baptism day arrived. I was doing my best to make the best of our lives together by not shutting down and hardening my heart, but it wasn't always easy. All the candidates for baptism had to share a few words before the congregation prior to going into the pool. When it was time for Manny to speak, he mentioned that I was his best friend and that he appreciated me being in his life. This had been the first time I had ever heard these words. As he spoke, he started to cry and I left my seat and went to stand with him. I wanted him to know that I had his back no

D.Nile Rivers

matter what we were going through. After he took a brief moment to gather himself, he was able to finish what he had to say. I was so proud of him. No one had any idea, that even at that moment, we were going through some serious changes and struggles as newlyweds.

Finding Mr. Right

Chapter Fifteen

Test of Faith

Approximately two days after Manny and I got baptized (August 2002), I got a call as I was about to leave work. It was Manny's boss calling to tell me that Manny had been taken to the emergency room. He said that Manny had a seizure and fainted. I laughed because I thought someone had the wrong number. I said, "My husband doesn't have seizures." He explained to me who he was and that it wasn't a joke. He told me where the ambulance had taken Manny. I thanked him and rushed out the door. When I got to the hospital and saw Manny, he was so relieved to see me. I could read it on his face. I greeted his family members who had arrived before me. I tried to get information about what happened, but it didn't make sense to me. Manny was confused. He told me that he had a seizure but he didn't remember having it or how he got to the hospital. I did my best to comfort him as I held his hand and told him that everything was going to be all right.

Eventually a nurse entered the room and asked everyone to leave. Manny held on to my hand and wouldn't let it go. I told the nurse that I was his wife, and she allowed me to stay. I took this opportunity to ask her what was going on. She told me that they were going to run tests on him. I took her aside and explained to her that Manny's doctor had taken tests and the results weren't back yet. I gave her the doctor's name and number and told her to get in touch with him. I also told her that I wanted every test they could think of done on Manny because something was obviously wrong.

Manny stayed in the hospital for five days. I continued to work during the day and saw him after work. Throughout this time, I had

85

D.Nile Rivers

contacted his doctor to find out if he had gotten the results of the tests they had taken months prior. He hadn't. He assured me that the hospital would do everything possible to find out what was wrong with Manny.

By the fifth day I got a call from a neurologist at the hospital. He told me that Manny had a brain tumor. At the time I got the call, I was on my way to pick up Morgan from the Boy's and Girl's Club. I had just gotten off work. I pulled the car over into their parking lot and listened in disbelief. I didn't want to believe it. I didn't understand how all of a sudden someone could just *have* a brain tumor. He said that because of the type of tumor Manny had, there was nothing they could do. He said that based on the CT-scans they had taken, the results showed that the tumor was a part of Manny's brain and it would be impossible to separate it.

When he finished talking, I was angry. I was angry with Manny for not telling me how sick he was before now. I thought, "There was no way he had made it this far without knowing something was wrong with him!"

I racked my brain trying to recall if there had been any signs or symptoms of Manny acting or looking sick. There was one time that he mentioned to me that he felt like he was having a nervous breakdown, but he wasn't specific. I would never have associated a nervous breakdown as a sign of a brain tumor. He never explained what made him think he was having a nervous breakdown.

Without knowing what to think or do, I prayed. Then I called Pastor and told him the news and he prayed. Eventually, every body in the church got involved in praying for Manny because he was greatly loved.

As word got around, people couldn't understand our reaction to the news. I did what I could to explain that my faith in God was keeping me from worrying. I told them exactly what I had told Manny, "Either God was going to heal him and it would be his testimony, or he was going to die." I prayed for healing, as did everyone else.

Because of our faith, we didn't walk around feeling sorry or in fear. At least I didn't. But I wasn't the one with the brain tumor. I thought Manny felt the same way, but I didn't know for sure because he didn't speak much. I decided to trust God and accept that His will would be done.

Manny only came to me once regarding what he was going

Finding Mr. Right

through. I tried to reassure him that God would work things out. I tried to comfort him and told him that everything would work out, that he should trust God. Somehow I don't think it was what he wanted to hear. I really didn't know what to tell him.

Once we told Manny's family about the brain tumor, we all agreed to get a second opinion regarding his situation. We were given the name of a neurosurgeon in Worcester, Massachusetts, and we made an appointment to see him.

On the day of the appointment, Manny's sister and father went along to hear what the doctor had to say. The doctor looked over Manny's x-rays and told us that he could perform a surgery to remove as much of the tumor as he could. He said that he performed this type of surgery regularly. He said that once he removed as much as he could of the tumor, Manny would have to go through radiation and chemotherapy.

It was something to think about, and we told him that we would let him know. It was a big decision to make, and no one could make it, but Manny.

Manny was placed on anti-seizure medicine and couldn't drive unless he was seizure free for six months. This meant that he needed someone to take him to and from work on a daily basis.

Manny's family and friends pitched in. It was a big help and an amazing demonstration of support. I knew it meant a lot to Manny. This also meant that there were people coming to the house that normally wouldn't. Manny even had one of his friends, who liked to cook, prepare meals for us every now and then. It was a nice touch. But, like with anything else, people grew tired and every now and then Manny would wake me up in the middle of the night to pick him up from work because no one was there to pick him up. I didn't mind because he was my husband, but he did because it meant I had to leave the kids in the house alone and he had to wake me up.

Somewhere between September (when we found out that Manny had a brain tumor) and December, things between Manny and I shifted for the worse. I didn't know it at the time, but it probably had a lot to do with what he was dealing with internally that I was not aware of. He was quiet by nature so it wasn't out of character for him to keep things from me. Naturally, I assumed that he was dealing with things. But this was not so.

Manny withdrew to the point where I grew frustrated and lashed

D.Nile Rivers

out at him. It didn't bother him. He simply ignored me, and with time we drifted further apart.

We got into a major argument one day, and I told him that I couldn't deal with things the way they were any more. I told him that we should go our separate ways. Manny agreed and contacted his sister to pick him up and take him to his mother's house.

I didn't know what to do, so I called Pastor. I told him what had happened, and he told me to come see him. While I was with Pastor, he explained to me that maybe the tumor was affecting Manny more than anyone realized. He explained that Manny could be experiencing fear and was afraid to express this to me. I hadn't thought about it like that. I just thought that Manny was being his usual self and ignoring me like he often did. I left Pastor's office with a different outlook. I still didn't know how to deal with him, but I was intent on trying to be more understanding.

I called Manny and explained to him what I was feeling. We talked things through, but even with our talk, he didn't change much. He came home and I tried to deal with things, but it wasn't easy. Dealing meant I had to live with someone who didn't speak to me. It was not a good feeling. I wanted him to speak to me, but I guess he just didn't know how.

If I had to place blame, I could say that maybe there was something I had shown him throughout the relationship that made him think that he couldn't speak to me. But Manny and I used to be such good friends. We used to share things with each other before and laugh and have fun. Not any more.

As we continued to go through and deal with each other in the best way we knew how, considering the circumstances, Manny remained withdrawn. Every now and then he would come back to reality, but it wasn't for long.

He continued to work and hang out with his family. It was a good thing because he got to catch up on things with people he didn't normally see, and he also took time to talk to them about Jesus.

The changes in him were obvious to many of his friends and family members. He was doing a good work even though he wasn't trying. It was a pleasure to see.

One day, out of the blue, I got a dozen long stemmed roses. Manny just stood there with a smile on his face as he watched the shock on my face. I had asked him to get me roses throughout the four

Finding Mr. Right

years we were together, and he never did. He didn't believe in giving me roses because he didn't want to do what had already been done in my previous relationships. Now, when I least expected it, I got roses for no particular reason other than to tell me that he loved me. He usually gave me cards to express how he felt, but this was special and unexpected.

As Christmas neared, things continued to be flaky between us; one minute we were on, and the next we were off. During one of our off weeks when Manny wasn't speaking to me, and I was frustrated and ready to quit altogether, I told him I wanted to go home to the Bahamas for vacation. I had never asked him for anything before. I wasn't the type of person to ask a man for money or felt that I needed anything from them, so this was a big step for me.

I was only able to be bold enough to ask because I was frustrated with the way things were between us. He thought it was a good idea and told me that he would get my ticket. I was thrilled to go because I hadn't been home in over twenty years. I needed the break. I needed to regroup in order to continue dealing with what I was going through.

I told Pastor about my trip when I saw him and he thought it was a good idea even though I hadn't asked him about it first. He asked about the situation on the home front, and I told him that it hadn't changed much. He asked if I wanted him to have a talk with the both of us, and I agreed to the meeting.

This wasn't the first time we had sought counseling. We had tried counseling previously in our relationship. Manny was never keen on going, but he went anyway.

Pastor made the arrangements with Manny and during our meeting, we were able to get some of our thoughts out. Pastor brought up the fact that a lot of the problem was relative to what Manny was going through internally. He also asked Manny about his part in the problem, and Manny confessed to cheating on me in the relationship. Somehow this had crept back into our relationship and was affecting us. I thought I had gotten past that, but in his silence, all sorts of thoughts were going through my head, including the past. I didn't know what to think!

Christmas came and Manny agreed to take care of Trey while I went on my ten-day trip home. He drove me to the airport in New York, even though he was prohibited from driving because of the seizure he had. He was on medication and had been seizure free. I

89

D.Nile Rivers

wanted to get someone else to drive me, but he insisted that he could do it.

We still weren't speaking to each other much so we rode in silence until I fell asleep. By the time I woke up, I was at the airport.

When I got to my homeland, I was in another world. I hadn't been there in so long. Things had changed, but at the same time remained the same. I was able to remember things and go places by myself even though I hadn't been there since I was twelve years old. It was great!

I did what I could not to focus on reality, but it wasn't easy. Even in the midst of my vacation, reality still reared its ugly head.

I tried to call Manny, but we kept playing phone tag. It wasn't until I actually spoke to him that he told me that my unit had been activated to go to Afghanistan, and I was being ordered by my Commander to fly back to the U.S.

I contacted my unit and explained to my Commander that I was out of the country on vacation. She didn't care. I hung up and prayed.

I half-heartedly tried to get a flight home, but was unable to because it was the holiday season and everything was booked. I was relieved. My Commander, on the other hand, was not happy to hear that. She told me to report to the unit upon my return.

Besides being concerned about going to war, I had a husband at home with a brain tumor who was in the process of trying to decided if he was going to have brain surgery or not. War was not my first priority. Regardless of what Manny and I were going through, this was still a major issue to deal with.

I had forgotten to mention to my Commander that Manny had a brain tumor and was in the process of trying to decide what to do about it. I knew that there was no way I was going to fight in a war when I had one already brewing at home.

Since I was unable to do anything where I was, Manny had to go around to the various doctors to provide my Commander with information as to why I couldn't go to Afghanistan. Manny was already nervous about having surgery and now even more so because he didn't want me to go to war. I didn't want to go either, but my reaction was, "God's will be done."

Based on the information Manny obtained regarding his health, my unit decided that I was unable to be shipped and we were able to relax a little.

When I returned from the trip, the first week of January, I reported

Finding Mr. Right

to my unit to assist in getting them ready to leave. I got permission to go home every night instead of staying at the unit so that I could be with Manny.

On one particular trip home, I called Manny to tell him that I was on my way, and in the middle of the conversation he started talking and not making any sense. Initially I thought that he had misunderstood what I had said, but the more we spoke, the more he didn't make sense. When I brought it to his attention, he didn't know what I was referring to. I realized that something was terribly wrong. When I got home, I immediately took him up to bed and made him lie down. I read the Bible to him as he laid his head on my stomach and listened. I prayed. I didn't know what else to do.

The next morning I called the neurologist and told him what had happened. He suggested that I bring him in as soon as possible. I told his family what happened and his sister and father decided to go with me to his appointment.

During the appointment, the doctor did some memory tests on Manny. As we watched and listened, we all became very aware that his illness had rapidly progressed.

It had only been four months since we found out, and the doctors had mentioned that the tumor could remain the way it was for ten to fifteen years. I didn't know what to think other than maybe it had already been ten or fifteen years since he had it. We were in shock. The doctor told us that a decision needed to be made about whether or not Manny was going have the surgery. It was a big decision, but it was one Manny had to make on his own. I couldn't tell him what to do.

The doctor explained the procedure that he would do, how long it would take, and the follow-up treatment. He repeated his explanation that he would remove as much of the tumor that he could and whatever remained would be treated with radiation or chemotherapy. He also told us that Manny would have problems with his short-term memory for a little while, but that it would get better.

Manny made up his mind that he would have the surgery, and a date was set for February 12th, 2003.

Manny's family and I sat down with him and came up with a plan. We decided that once he had the surgery, his stepmother would take care of him, which meant he would stay with her while I continued to work. I suggested that I would come over every day after work and

91

bathe him and spend time with him until it was time for me to go back home. I also decided that I would be the one to take him to his appointments and radiation treatments when they started. Manny was cool with the arrangements, even though he didn't say much.

On the day of the surgery, things between Manny and I were still not well. We still weren't speaking like we should. We had grown apart, and there wasn't much to say, but I wanted him to know that I was there. His family wasn't there at the time he went in to surgery. I wished we had more to say. I wished things were different, but they weren't. I gave him his Bible, and he was off. The nurse told me the approximate time I would have to wait and where I should wait.

When Manny's family arrived, we waited patiently for him to come out of surgery. I read my Bible and was in good spirits because I trusted that God was going to bring him through. Even though his family was there, I spent the majority of the time by myself.

The surgery took a little longer than they expected. When the doctor came to us, he told us that he had removed as much of the tumor as he could and that he had sent a sample to the lab for analysis. He told us that it would take four days for the results to come back. I didn't understand why it would take so long, but that is what we were told.

It was evening when I finally got to see Manny and almost time for me to get home to the kids. I had been there since early morning. Manny's older brother Junior had arrived with a friend, and we were all let into the recovery room to see him. We were told that we couldn't stay long, but I didn't want to leave.

When I first saw him, the numbness that had taken up residence in my heart, went away. He looked so helpless. To look at him you would think he was sound asleep, but I knew better. He didn't open his eyes at first, but I knew he was awake because when I held his hand, he held mine back.

I whispered in his ear that it was me and that he was going to be fine. I told him all the things I hadn't told him before the surgery: that I loved him and I needed him. I did what I could to reassure him that he was going to be okay.

When he finally opened his eyes, he looked at me as if he didn't know me at first, but it was just a matter of adjustment. His look was intense and his grip just as intense. He looked at me questioningly and I asked, "What do YOU want?" We hadn't spoken to each other in

Finding Mr. Right

such a long time. We were like strangers. Things seemed different, almost desperate. His answer to my question was, "I want my wife!" I held on to his hand and I looked him in his eyes and said, "I'm here. You got me." I don't know if the words registered with him or not, but he kept saying, "I want my wife." It took everything I could not to cry. I wanted to continue to act like I was built of stone and unfazed by all that had happened between us. But I had been fazed. I had been hurting. I looked at him again and I said, "I am here. You got me."

I did what I could to make him feel comfortable. The nurse came by and explained to me what was going on and what they were doing. I stayed as long as I could, and when I had to leave, he wouldn't let go of my hand. It tugged at me because it gave me hope. I made up in my mind then and there that I was going to do whatever it took to make things work between us.

As I was leaving, I bumped into Pastor and his wife on their way to see Manny. I filled them in and agreed to watch their children in the waiting room while they went in to visit. They were in there a while, and when they came out, Pastor told me that Manny couldn't stop talking about me and how much my words had meant to him. I was surprised that he had said anything at all because I didn't realize I had done anything to warrant the praise. But it felt good to know that he had listened and was aware that I was there for him.

For the remainder of Manny's stay in the hospital, the focus was on his short-term memory and being able to walk and eat. He didn't know my name or anyone else's, but he was aware of who people were.

The doctor said that his memory would come back to him over time and that he would have therapy for it. In addition to his memory being shaky, he seemed to have trouble with his right side. He wasn't able to hold things in his right hand and his right foot dragged when he walked. In other words, he acted like someone who had a stroke. The doctor and nurses didn't seem too concerned and told us that he would have physical therapy once he was able to.

When Manny was released from the hospital, he went to his stepmother, Dee's like we agreed. He was given a follow-up appointment in two weeks. He was to receive physical therapy in the meantime.

As agreed, when I finished work everyday, I went to Dee's house to bathe him and spend time with him. It was something that I wanted to do, and I was glad to do it, but I didn't expect what I got. Manny

93

D.Nile Rivers

went back to not speaking to me. He spoke to everyone else who spoke to him, but whenever I asked him something he wouldn't actually open his mouth to speak. He would simply nod or shake his head. I didn't say anything because I knew his memory wasn't up to speed, but as I watched him interact with visitors and his family, I realized that he was just that way with me. I decided to overlook it and prayed that it would get better in time.

Within the first week of being at Dee's, I realized that she had a problem with me. I didn't know why, but she started to ignore me, and when she did speak, she was mean. Manny picked up on this, but still wouldn't speak.

Manny was constantly being bombarded with phone calls. It didn't matter if he was asleep; Dee would wake him up to talk knowing his memory wasn't altogether there. Manny didn't say anything about it.

If Manny wasn't dealing with the constant phone calls, then it was the friction between Dee and me. I did what I could to stay out of her way and just spend time with him.

One day, after giving Manny his bath, he started to cry. Dee and I were still not getting along and it showed. This was obviously upsetting him. He couldn't explain to me why he was upset, so I asked him, "Do you want to go home?" He nodded his head in agreement. I told him that I would take him home when the weekend came. I knew Dee wasn't going to be happy with this change of plan, but it wasn't about her.

Dee told the therapist that Manny was in a good environment. She told the therapist that he was being taken care of and that he was getting all the rest he needed. I stood there in disbelief as I listened to her lies.

Every time I went to take care of him after work, instead of him being able to rest, he was constantly being awakened to speak to someone calling to ask how he was doing and wanting to chat. All this did was add to the headaches he was already having because it required a lot for him to think and try to remember people. I tried to talk to Dee, but it didn't matter what I said because it wasn't my house.

I wanted to get him out of there and I told him that I would, but I also knew that I had to work. I decided to get my family involved, and they all got together and decided to bring Mom, who was now living in the Bahamas, to the U.S. to help take care of Manny while I worked.

I contacted the therapist and explained to her what kind of environ-

94

Finding Mr. Right

ment Manny was in and told her that he wanted to come home. By the end of the week and with the help of the therapist, I got Manny home.

I brought our bed down to the first floor so he wouldn't have to go up the stairs. I also brought the things he would need downstairs and made them easily accessible.

I took the week off from work, but in the back of my mind, I still wanted to be at work because I needed to make money for us to live. I told him I wanted to work and had planned on getting someone to take care of him, but in the end, I decided to stay home. He didn't want anyone else taking care of him.

By day three, things were looking good. Manny continued to do his therapy and started lifting little hand weights. He still didn't speak much, but I was able to understand what he wanted. I continued to bathe him, but I was only able to feed him when he let me. He was determined to make his right hand work. And even though he was hardly able to feed himself, he decided to feed me one day. It is something I will never forget. He wasn't speaking to me much, but he wanted to let me know that he was trying by doing something for me. It was priceless and spoke more words than he could ever say.

Manny's family was upset with me because I had taken him home to be with me. Of course, it was my fault! His brother Junior didn't mind the move because he wasn't close to the family and didn't like going over there anyway. Instead, he came to my house, and it was fine with us. He came to see how Manny was doing, and he actually got to catch him laughing while watching a scene from *The Nutty Professor* one day while he was visiting.

Manny seemed more comfortable being home than at Dee's house. He even wanted to have sex in his condition. I didn't know if it was a good idea, but apparently something was still working right.

By day five of being home, Manny started to get upset. He kept complaining that his head hurt. I contacted his doctor, but he said it was to be expected. I gave him his medication and something to relieve his pain, but nothing worked.

I took Manny to his appointment for a radiation consultation later that same day. At this point, I still didn't know Manny had cancer. I knew they had removed a tumor from his brain, but no one had ever mentioned the word "cancer" since the surgery or thereafter. When the doctor entered the room to talk to us he said, "So how is he? Does he appear to be better?"

95

D.Nile Rivers

I looked at him and said, "No, he seems worse than before the surgery."

I explained to him how he walked as if he had a stroke and that his memory hadn't improved, etc. I told him that he hadn't had a follow-up appointment with the neurologist. I told him that when we arrived at the hospital for the follow-up after the surgery, the doctor was on vacation and no one else saw him in regards to how he was doing. I told him that all they did was remove the stitches from his head. This doctor seemed concerned and decided to do an exam of Manny himself. He checked the movement in his leg and his arm. He checked his heart and anything else he could think of, and then he looked over the notes he had received pertaining to the surgery. He began speaking and saw that I wasn't following. He explained that the surgeon had removed the left temporal lobe, which would explain the lack of movement on his right side. I looked at him in shock. I didn't know.

The surgeon had said that they were going to remove as much of the tumor as they could, not the left part of his brain. I was angry. Manny didn't say anything. The doctor then said that Manny had cancer and that was the purpose for the radiation, which is what we were there to discuss. I should have known he had cancer simply because he was going to have radiation, but I had never been close to someone in a situation like this, so I didn't know any better. In my mind, I just knew that they removed as much of the tumor that they could, and they were going to get the rest by using radiation.

The doctor was very nice and very helpful. He explained what was going to happen in the following weeks and explained why they had to wait a little while because he had just had the surgery two weeks prior. I thanked him and left.

When we got out in the hallway, Manny was upset. He couldn't really say what he wanted to, but I understood. What he tried to say was that he thought he was okay now that they had done the surgery. I told him, "No." As I helped him walk, I saw the expression on his face. He was so sad, but he was also in pain. He told me that he wasn't feeling well, and when I asked him if he wanted to go home, he shook his head, "Yes."

We slowly walked out of the building and I told him to wait for me by the sidewalk while I went to get the car. When I got him in the car, I drove straight home.

Finding Mr. Right

Manny had an appointment with the physical therapist later on in the day, but he said that he didn't want to because he wasn't feeling well. He indicated to me that his head hurt. When the therapist arrived, Manny refused to cooperate with the therapist, and she eventually left.

Manny woke up around nine that evening and threw up the medication I gave him. He just seemed to be getting worse. It wasn't until he went to the bathroom (he wanted to go by himself) and said, "It's blue." I didn't know what he was talking about at first, but then realized that he was referring to his urine. I didn't think he was saying exactly what he meant to say, so I showed him an object with the colors red and blue on it. He pointed to the red and kept saying blue. That was it! I called his doctor, and he told me to take him to the emergency room where we lived. I explained to the physician at the emergency room that he had thrown up, and there was blood in his urine. They admitted him and gave him medication for the pain. I stayed with him as long as I could and then I left around eleven to check on the children.

I checked on the children, got some of his clothes together in case he needed them, and headed back to the hospital. When I got there, Manny wasn't around. I was told that he had been taken to get a CT-scan. I waited until he returned, and they informed me that there was a large mass on the left side of his head. I listened in disbelief. It had only been a little over two weeks, and it had returned. I didn't even know this was a possibility. They informed me that they were going to transfer him to Worcester, where he had the surgery done, because they were more familiar with his case.

Manny didn't want me to tell anyone that he was going back in the hospital. I begged him to let me call someone in his family to let them know, and he finally agreed to let me call Junior. I immediately called his brother and told him the news. I explained to him that he didn't want anyone to know because he didn't want to deal with the animosity between his stepmother and me or any stress. He agreed with me, and we left it at that.

I stayed with Manny for as long as I could into the wee hours of the morning. I had to get back home to the children to make sure they got up on time for school. I kissed him and told him that I would be there as soon as I got the children off to school and left.

When I got to the hospital later on that morning, he was doing

D.Nile Rivers

much better. When I saw him, he was sitting up in bed and appeared to be fine. There was no doctor around and when asked, the nurses told me that they were going to run tests, etc.

As the day progressed, I stayed with Manny. I asked him if I could call his family, and he wouldn't allow it. I did call Junior to let him know that we were in Worcester.

Manny ate the food they gave him, and I read to him to pass the time. Pastor came to visit and they had a good time together. He seemed to be doing all right. When it was time to leave, I told him that I would see him the following day.

The next day was not so promising. Manny was very angry when I arrived. He was in pain. His eyes were red, and he was extremely irritable. I harassed the nurses until they gave him pain medicine to help with the pain. When he took the pills, he threw them up. No one did or said anything.

Manny tried to sleep, but he kept waking up because of the pain in his head. I kept telling the nurses that he was in pain. They claimed that they contacted his doctor who told them to check the fluid in his brain. They took a sample of spinal fluid to check for infection.

Every time I saw someone I asked what the results of the tests were, but no one could tell me. When a resident came to check on him, I asked her if it was normal for one side of his forehead to be cold and the other hot. She guessed that maybe one of his nerves on that side of his head was cut during the surgery and it could cause the cold/heat that I referred to.

No one really knew anything, but at the same time, no one seemed concerned or took things seriously as if he was in any danger.

I had been there a good portion of the day and was having a hard time with the fact that his doctor had not shown up. When he did call and I got a chance to speak to him, he told me that the mass had grown back and they were running tests, but he never seemed concerned or shared with me that Manny was in danger.

Manny slept most of the day. When he was awake, he was angry and in pain. At one point the pain got so bad that he sat straight up in the bed and screamed, "My head!" I begged them to give him something more for the pain.

At this point, I called Dee and told her that Manny was back in the hospital. I explained to her that he had arrived the day before, and I hadn't called her because he didn't want me to. I told her that Junior

Finding Mr. Right

knew, and he had agreed with me as well. She was not happy with me, but said that she would come out the next day.

The next day was Saturday. I was on my way to the hospital, but I had to make a stop at the church first. As I got to the church, Manny's doctor called.

He said, "Manny is almost in a coma."

"What are you talking about? I just saw him last night."

"His eyes are dilated and he's almost unresponsive."

"What does that mean?"

"It doesn't look good."

"What are you saying?"

"Manny is dying."

"Can't you do another surgery?"

"I could, but I wouldn't recommend it because he would be a vegetable."

I hung up the phone, looked at my son in the seat next to me, and I told him that Manny was dying. I parked the car and ran into the church where they were having prayer.

I walked up to the altar in tears. I couldn't hold it in. I told them that Manny was dying, and they prayed for me and for him.

As they prayed, I had a vision of myself being in the hospital and lying outstretched on top of Manny on his hospital bed. I heard myself saying, "Flesh of my flesh, blood of my blood." I saw it as clearly as it was given to me. I didn't really understand, but I felt like I was supposed to do what I had seen. So I had my hands anointed with oil. I called Pastor and told him that Manny was almost in a coma, and he asked me to wait for him at the church.

We drove to the hospital together, still believing that God was going to deliver him. I called my sister, Lovey, and she told me that she would meet me at the hospital. I called Junior and he passed the word. I called my mentor and he came as well.

When we got to the hospital, Manny was incoherent. He had the ability to move one of his arms, but aside from that, he wasn't with us. It didn't look good. As I spoke to him in his ear, Pastor and the rest of people prayed. And as they prayed, I did my best to believe that he would make it through. He didn't.

Later on that same day, Manny's breathing became labored to the point where his entire body rocked as he breathed. The nurses came and went and no one seemed concerned. I finally asked one of them,

D.Nile Rivers

"Why is he breathing like that? Is that normal?" She said, "I don't know. I'll see if I can get someone to check his blood to see if he is getting enough oxygen." I still believed, at this point, that he would be healed. And still, I hadn't seen his doctor.

Lovey arrived and was there as my support. Manny's dad arrived with Manny's son. Junior was there as well.

Manny's blood had been taken prior to their arrival. I explained to them that they were checking his blood to see if he was getting enough oxygen because I was concerned about his breathing. Before they came back with the results, and while I was yet talking to them, Manny took a deep breath and stopped breathing. I screamed, "NO!"

This wasn't happening. I pressed the button for help while trying to open Manny's mouth to do rescue breathing. He still had a pulse. As I looked at his face, I saw a tear roll down his cheek. A nurse came in, and I told her that he wasn't breathing. She decided to take the time to check his blood pressure. I told her, "He's not breathing!" At that same time, someone was speaking to me on a speaker from the nurse's desk, asking me if there was an emergency. I told her that Manny had stopped breathing.

A 'stat' was finally called, and Lovey whisked me out of the room so that the nurses and doctors could do what they had to do to save Manny's life. I already knew he was gone.

In the hallway, I cried like I had lost my heart as Lovey held me. Secretly, I asked God to save him.

I wasn't able to see Manny for a while. They needed to intubate him, and hook him up to machines and drips, etc. Why hadn't they done this before? Didn't they know that he was critical before I asked them about his breathing? I was angry, but I didn't want to appear "un-Christian."

Someone came to me and informed me that they had contacted his doctor. Oh, the same doctor I hadn't seen in the three days since Manny had been back in the hospital? The same doctor who didn't think it necessary to inform us that Manny was critical; that the mass had grown back and had taken over his brain?

When the doctor finally approached me, he said, "It doesn't look good. There is no brain activity." He said, "I can place a shunt in his head to try to reduce the swelling but it doesn't look good." I looked at him in disbelief. He said, "Manny is brain dead. I can pronounce him brain dead now, but I'll give him twenty-four hours before I take him

Finding Mr. Right

off the respirator." Imagine my disbelief. All they could tell me was that he would have been dead soon anyway based on how quickly he had progressed. I didn't want to hear that nonsense.

Lovey stayed as long as she could. Manny's father, brother and son left shortly after Lovey. It was just Manny and me. They had moved him to the ICU and had him hooked up to all sorts of machines. It was extremely hard for me to look at him without crying. When I held his hand, it was cold as death. I knew he wasn't alive, but I kept praying and asking God to wake him up and to heal him. I spent the night with him, talking to him and looking for any signs of movement, but there was none.

When morning came, Manny's family arrived, and they looked through me as if I didn't exist. Eventually Lovey and her family arrived. Mom was there as well for support. The treatment I received from Manny's family hurt, but not as badly as losing Manny.

When we gave the go ahead to turn off the ventilator, I couldn't be there to see it. I had already said my farewell throughout the night. His family thought I was cold, but they hadn't been there with me all night to know what I went through, nor did they care. I was unable to speak, so Lovey took over and dealt with the family regarding funeral arrangements and such.

Once Manny was buried, things with his family didn't get any better. It never dawned on me that they would be the way they were or would do the things that they did. All I could do was pray and ask God for strength. There was nothing more I could do.

In dealing with the hospital and trying to get answers, I did what I could, but I got nowhere. All I really wanted was an explanation. Why didn't they prepare us by telling us that Manny was terminal once he had been readmitted to the hospital? Why didn't the doctor tell us once he had done the surgery that Manny only had three weeks to live? So many questions, and they weren't giving any answers.

I fell back on my law enforcement skills and decided to conduct an investigation. I requested all Manny's files from all the doctors he had seen. I went on the internet and researched the type of tumor Manny had and its symptoms, etc. I researched all the medications he was taking. When I started asking questions and requesting records, the doctors, all of a sudden, became unavailable. When I did get to speak to them, they were vague or inquired as to why I needed the records. Suddenly, everyone was trying to cover their tracks. When I went to

101

D.Nile Rivers

the hospital to get Manny's x-ray, they conveniently couldn't be found even though I had requested them in advance. After waiting for almost an hour, I was told that his records were being reviewed by medical staff.

I contacted cancer doctors with questions about Manny's medical records and explanations of tests results, etc. I told them about his rapid weight loss, bouts of disorientation, and issues with his left eye prior to his tumor diagnosis. I learned that all the symptoms I described were side effects to the tumor he had on the left temporal lobe. Unfortunately, I was learning all this too late.

Manny's autopsy results showed that he died from swelling on the brain. According to the side effects of the medication Manny was on after his surgery, brain swelling was one of them. If the surgeon knew the medication would cause Manny's brain to swell, why wasn't he available for Manny's follow-up appointment after the surgery? Why was he on vacation and didn't make any alternate plans for Manny to see another doctor? If the surgeon knew that the type of tumor Manny had would more than likely grow back within a short period of time, why didn't he inform us of this once the surgery was done? I could only conclude that Manny was used as a guinea pig. I couldn't find any other explanation and no one was giving me anything else to go on except the fact that Manny would have been dead any way.

I spoke to patient administration and the patient advocate regarding my concerns. When I explained to them that no one had told me that Manny had cancer, they were surprised.

They asked, "Did anyone sit down with you and inform you about the procedures for patients with cancer and what to expect?"

"No, I replied. I didn't even know Manny had cancer until after the fact."

The woman I spoke to understood my concern and told me to contact the Board of Health with my questions.

By the time I was through with my investigation, I had a twenty-four page report. I submitted it to the Board of Health in the form of a complaint, but their response was that my complaint was unfounded. They stated that the surgeon didn't violate any rights. I was angry. I knew Manny had not been treated fairly, but I couldn't get anyone to accept the responsibility.

I went to five different attorneys with my case. I told them that I needed help in getting the hospital to answer my questions, but they

Finding Mr. Right

wouldn't take the case. They all told me that the time frame from when Manny was first diagnosed, and when he died was too short a time span. Meaning, Manny would have died when he did anyway.

Nothing anyone said to me could convince me that Manny wasn't treated fairly. Even if Manny was dying, they should have told us so we could have prepared for his death.

I eventually gave up because the longer I carried on the fight, the longer it took me to grieve. But I didn't want to let go because it wasn't fair what they had done or how they had treated him. I didn't want Manny to think that I didn't fight for him, but I couldn't do it any more.

Chapter Sixteen

The Aftermath

Picking up the pieces after Manny passed away wasn't what I or anyone had expected. I didn't take any time off from work, and I didn't lose my mind like I thought I would. Instead, I came to the reality that Manny was gone and he wouldn't be coming back.

I knew in my heart and mind that no amount of time away from work was going to make a difference, at least not at the point where I was. I also knew that his memory would always be with me because everywhere I looked I had a memory of him doing something or being somewhere. Even though he was gone, in my heart, he was very much alive.

I stayed in prayer, and I sought comfort and answers from God because I needed to understand what I was supposed to get from losing Manny so soon. In the midst of dealing with Manny's family and their hatred toward me, and trying to process what actually happened, I received a revelation from the Holy Spirit. I learned that Manny had been an assignment. This was something new to me. I contacted my mentor and told him what I had learned. When I said it to him, there was silence on the other end of the phone. He told me that this had been previously revealed to him, but he wasn't able to speak to me about it. I'm sure he did this because I wouldn't have understood.

As we spoke, he explained to me exactly what "assignment" meant, and as a result, I went to God in prayer hoping that he was pleased with me.

With the funeral over, I no longer had any dealings with Manny's family. Actually, I should say that his family no longer had any dealings with me. At first, I was hurt, but I eventually learned that it was better if I had nothing to do with them at all. They were angry

Finding Mr. Right

with me because they didn't get to see him before he died, but that was due to their own stubbornness. I told them he was back in the hospital and they came when they wanted to. Granted, none of us knew he was going to die.

As time went by, I had unexpected moments when I would break down and cry. I didn't like those moments because I had no control over them, and I was so set on giving the appearance that I was in control. I only wanted to have those moments when I was alone.

I wasn't the only one who had those moments. I had a co-worker try to visit me at work, and she just broke down when she saw me.

It was apparent that the effect of Manny's death went far beyond what I had imagined. The outreach and support from my co-workers was incredible! I really didn't know Manny and I had touched so many lives. The love was amazing and encouraging all at the same time. It allowed me to realize just how important it was to be aware of the people we come in contact with because we don't know the effect we might have on them.

Eventually, I ended up going through an angry stage. I was angry with Manny for leaving me, even though I knew he had nothing to do with *when* he went. There was so much we didn't say and so much we needed to clear up, but it was too late. I knew that Manny was in a better place and free from the pain he was going through. But I wasn't through with him yet. All I could do was pray and ask God for strength and understanding.

There were days when I would be fine, and there were days when I just had to walk out of my job and tell my boss I needed a moment. She was very understanding and accommodating.

Eventually, I got to the point where I could think about him without losing control and instead, I just smiled because I realized that I still had the memories we had made. Manny wasn't with me physically, but he lived on in the memories of what used to be.

I continued to go to church, and I praised God more than I ever had. I praised him for preparing me before Manny's death and even more so for keeping me now that he was gone. But people at church didn't understand my rejoicing and my praises to God. They expected me to be distraught and to be a complete mess. As a result of my not living up to their expectations, I was talked about. They assumed and commented behind my back that I didn't love Manny because I wasn't grieving enough. It bothered me a little to hear that, but what I

D.Nile Rivers

eventually ended up asking people was, "Are you praying for me?"
They would say, "Yes".

I would then say, "Then your prayers have been answered."

It was obvious that they didn't believe that their prayers would be answered or maybe they expected them to be answered in another way. Regardless, they had no idea what I was going through or had already been through.

I was made aware of many things during this time and the months to come. Pastor and my mentor kept in touch regularly as well as other close members in the church. My family was readily available as well.

In talking to Pastor one day, he encouraged me to write about how I felt and my testimony. I hadn't thought of it, but once I prayed about it, I was led to write "The Spoken Word" newsletter. In it I was able to share with others, who might be going through or have gone through similar experiences, words of encouragement.

Writing about my experience in dealing with Manny's death enabled me, to some extent, to share some of my feelings. What I didn't realize was that I had suppressed many of my feelings in order to move on, not knowing that in suppressing them, I was only prolonging my grief. I had convinced myself that I would deal with my grief in stages, when I was able to fully handle it.

Since I was dealing with my grief, by not dealing with my grief, I went on with life as usual. I continued to do what I normally would, but added more onto my plate as an attempt to deflect my focus from Manny. Whatever came my way, if it was something that interested me, I did. If someone wanted me to get involved in something in the church, I did. If there was a function going on at church, I was there. I was going full steam ahead.

One day I decided to take a trip to Maryland to visit my sister. I needed to get away to regroup; something I did when I felt overwhelmed or when I needed to refocus. As I headed out, I decided to give Chief a call to see how he was doing. I told him that I was going to be passing through his neck of the woods and wanted to know if he had some time for a visit. I gave him a brief synopsis of my life up to that point and he offered his condolences regarding Manny's passing.

He was up for the visit and we made plans to meet. We decided to meet at the usual restaurant.

I was actually excited about seeing him again. Five years had gone

106

Finding Mr. Right

by and I had no idea how things would be between us. I didn't know if that chemistry would still be there or how he would react. It didn't really matter because I was saved and living for Christ now, so it was a different story. I wasn't looking for anything, but I didn't expect what I got either.

Chief looked the same – Great! He hadn't changed a bit, and apparently, neither did his feelings or attraction for me. I was surprised because it had been years, and yet he still felt the same for me. I, on the other hand, didn't feel a thing for him physically. I still loved him dearly because of our history, but our meeting was simply an act of catching up and seeing him again.

We talked and got caught up on what we had both missed. He didn't have a lot of time to visit because he had to pick up his kids from childcare. He now had two little girls.

I hated to leave. Being with him was comforting. He didn't want me to leave either. When we finally got up to go our separate ways, we hugged to say our farewells. It felt so safe and familiar to me. To him, it was more than that, if you know what I mean. Chief always carried a gun because of work, but I didn't think that was what I felt in his front pocket when he hugged me.

He made an attempt to kiss me, and I pulled back and looked at him in surprise. I reminded him, "You're married." He didn't want to hear that. He was still unhappy in his relationship with his wife and he didn't mind telling me about it. But I also reminded him that I was saved and took it seriously. He didn't want to hear that either.

He finally let me go and as hard as it was to leave, I got in my car. As I pulled away from the curb, he called me on my cell and asked me to meet him around the corner for a minute. When I got out the car to talk to him, he held me again, and I let him. My flesh wanted to feel *something* but it wasn't there. I knew God was totally in control and not allowing anything to happen because it would be a distraction, not to mention, wrong.

As he hugged me, I thought about Manny and how he had cheated on me. I tried to put myself in his wife's shoes, and I knew that even though my hugs to him were innocent in my mind, they weren't in his, and I had to tell him to let me go. He tried to talk me into giving in to him, but I just couldn't do it, nor did I feel it. I finally got back in my car and went on my way.

He and I kept in touch after that encounter. Every time we spoke,

D.Nile Rivers

we spoke of the past, which only led to his frustration. I eventually found the nerve to tell him how badly he had hurt me when he got married and how listening to his escapades all these years about all his flings had hurt me. He wasn't very sympathetic, and that was expected. He took the time to vent as well and shared with me how I had hurt him by not having the child for him that he had wanted. I didn't realize that he had actually been serious at the time and shared that with him. Either way, we both vented and got things out, but it didn't change a thing.

We tried to meet a couple times after that initial meeting, but as God would have it, something always came up. Each time I smiled and told God, "Good one."

He and I both knew that it was divine intervention stepping in every time, but it didn't stop us from trying. And just as clearly as I knew it was God, I heard the Holy Spirit say one day, "You have to let him go." I didn't want to hear that at all! We had been friends for so long! He had been a part of my life for so many years that I didn't want to let him go. I could live without seeing him, but I didn't want to stop communicating with him, even if it was just a few times a year.

But disobedience has its consequences. On two more occasions we met, and on each one he got into a car accident, which nearly totaled his cars. He ended up with no car and financially stressed. The next time I spoke to him, he verbally took things out on me because he couldn't take it out on his wife. I listened and cringed as he made me feel lower than the ground itself. When he was through cursing me out and belittling me, I simply hung up the phone and cried like a baby. I was in shock! I couldn't believe the things he had said or the way he had spoken to me. I convinced myself that he needed to take it out on someone, so it might as well have been me since he knew I would forgive him. No sooner than the words left his lips, I did just that. But still, it was totally unexpected and hurtful.

I didn't speak to him for months after that. I kept waiting for him to apologize, but he never did. When I finally spoke to him again, he basically told me to get over it. It bothered me that he could be so cold, but I didn't have to deal with him if I didn't want to, so I let it go.

For him, nothing had changed, and it was business as usual between us. We would catch up on each other's lives and reflect on the past from time to time. Aside from that, it was nothing. There was nothing to have. He was still married, and I was still not feeling him.

Finding Mr. Right

But for some reason I didn't want to let go of the past. It wasn't until he said to me one day, "Did you ever think that maybe you just need to let me go?" that I remembered that I was supposed to do just that. I couldn't believe what he said because it just confirmed what I was already told. I told him that I was aware of that, but that I wasn't able to do it. He advised me that I should. I said nothing in return. He was my "Mr. Right," and as far as I was concerned, I would remain alone or continue to marry other people because I wasn't his "Mrs. Right." It didn't matter that in my heart I couldn't let go.

I didn't let him go completely, but I did stop communicating with him to some extent. I realized that we never really had anything to talk about aside from him being miserable in his marriage and us reminiscing about the past. It got old and unnecessary.

A year went by, and we pretty much left each other alone. We emailed once in a blue moon, but for the most part there was nothing more to do.

Within that same year, I met someone and eventually shared this with Chief who couldn't believe it and had something to say about it. Why did I call him? Because it was something I was used to doing. For some reason I still wanted to keep him in my life, even though I knew better.

In 2005, about a year after I was involved in my new relationship, I received an email from Chief telling me that he no longer thought we needed to communicate with each other. He said that he was going to focus on his relationship with God and he was going to deal with his commitment to his marriage.

I was happy for him, but I couldn't understand why he and I couldn't remain friends. He said, "Being friends with you is comparable to an alcoholic in a liquor store." I understood what he meant simply because of how he responded when he saw me, etc., but I couldn't agree to never see or talk to him again. I simply emailed him back and said, "O.K." I wanted to say more, but I was so hurt; I just didn't know how to respond otherwise.

It took a few months for me to get past the hurt and chew him out for being so cold even though I knew he was doing the right thing.

Bottom line, he was my idea of Mr. Right. It didn't matter that I was fully aware of all his dirt over the years and the fact that I knew we wouldn't work out even if he were single. I still wanted to hold on to our past together. But God was in control, and He knew I wasn't

109

D.Nile Rivers

going to do it on my own, so He did it for me.

I later realized that I was nothing more than a memory to Chief that he replayed in his mind from time to time; memories of us that would be considered adultery in the eyes of God, and anyone else for that matter. But he was more to me than a memory; he was a feeling in my heart. But like memories do, they fade and are forgotten. My feelings for him weren't that easy to dismiss. I was able to find comfort with this understanding of where I fit into his life after all these years. I was able to finally understand how he could so easily cut me off without a second thought. Though I understood, I was still hurt. I had wasted so many years cherishing what we had shared only to find out that it was one-sided. But with the help of God, I was able to ask for deliverance from whatever it was that kept me bound to him and for help to move on from this chapter in my life.

Chapter Seventeen

"Divine" Intervention

April of 2004, the church was nearing the end of a forty-day fast. This was my first forty-day fast, and I had determined in my mind that I was going to make it to the end. Some of the things on the list to pray for included financial blessings, for God to bring single, saved men and women into the church, healing, etc. It was my first time, so I did as I was directed and basically prayed for everything on the list. I had other requests like, strength, patience, endurance, direction, wisdom, etc.

During the fast, I was directed by the Holy Spirit to anoint myself each day, from head to foot (and everywhere in between) with anointed, virgin olive oil. I was not allowed to wear any lotions, perfumes, or anything other than the oil. I smelled like "a walking olive." You could have thrown me in the pot and made some stir-fry. I didn't like smelling like olive oil all day, or leaving grease everywhere I touched, but I was obedient. I didn't understand the reasoning behind what I was doing, and I didn't ask. At this point in my life I was more concerned with being obedient to God than asking questions.

When the fast ended, I had a discussion with a few sisters from the church. In the midst of our discussion, we began to share our experiences during the fast and some of the things that we were led to do. One of the sisters shared a story in which she was in bed asleep one night only to be awakened by someone being on top of her. She said that she thought it was a dream except when she opened her eyes no one was there, and she could still feel as if someone was on top of her. She explained the sensations she felt and how real it was. As she shared, the other sister chimed in to explain that she also had a similar experience. As I listened, it was revealed to me why I was directed to

D.Nile Rivers

anoint myself every day during my fast.

I had been told previously about a sexual demon that was present in the church. At the time I didn't think anything of it, but as I listened to what was being said, the knowledge was brought to my memory. The experience these sisters had could very easily have happened to me had I not been covered from head to toe as directed.

The devil knew sex was a sure way of getting me to sin against God. It had worked in the past, and even though he knew that I was determined to serve God, it wasn't going to stop him from trying to mess me up.

He sent a couple temptations my way in the form of physically attractive men who pretended to be Godly. One quoted the Bible like it was a second language and did what he could to persuade me to sleep with him, but it didn't work. I explained to him that I took my salvation seriously, and I wasn't trying to mess things up by being disobedient. I reminded him that sex before marriage was a sin. He had a counter-attack for that. He said that we didn't need a piece of paper to state that we were married. He said that man created the piece of paper for public satisfaction, and that back in the days of the Old Testament, when a man chose a wife he simply went before God and presented her as his wife.

Well, I couldn't believe what I heard. I had to take another look at this man to see if he was serious. He was, and to prove how serious he was, he made a vow to God taking me to be his wife. When he was finished, he told me to do the same and stated that once I had, it would be okay in the sight of God for us to have sex. Wow! I had to laugh at that. The devil was very clever, but thank God I knew what the Bible said and was able to pass on his offer.

This same Bible-quoting individual had every excuse why he didn't want to go to church. But even with this test, time was passing by, and God knew that it was just a matter of time before the devil would play the "sex card" again.

What my sisters experienced during their fast could easily have happened to me. My sexual desires would have been aroused, thus tempting me to do something I had no business doing. So, though I didn't understand the reasons behind why I had anointed myself, God knew. Thank God for His divine intervention.

That wasn't the devil's only attempt. Later that same year, around summer time, I went to the Bahamas to get away from my life. I had

Finding Mr. Right

no expectations other than to relax and have some quality "me" time. Well, the devil had expectations as well—to tempt me and make me fall.

Once I was there, I started spending time with someone I considered my big brother. We didn't know each other well because it had been over twenty years since we had seen each other or had even thought of each other. He was now a grown man with a wife and kids.

He and I hit it off instantly. The more we talked, the more we realized how alike we were. We could have been carbon copies of each other with the exception of our genders. It was a nice feeling, to have someone who understood me. As a result, I was always at his home spending time with him and his family. There was such a welcoming atmosphere at his home. The way the kids interacted with each other and the chemistry between everyone in the house was something I wished I had growing up. The more time I spent with them, the more I felt a part of the family, and at the time, I was at a place in my life where I needed that.

It wasn't long before his wife mentioned to me that we should be careful about spending too much time together. She told us that we shouldn't try to catch up on twenty years in one visit. I didn't see what the problem was. I was just happy that I had someone I could talk to that understood me and accepted me for who I was. But I had to learn the hard way or maybe it wasn't that I "had" to learn the hard way.

Before you knew it, we had spent so much time together that we developed feelings for each other that we couldn't explain. I tried to explain to his wife how I felt, but she didn't understand. She didn't understand the bond that had formed between us in such a short period of time.

He on the other hand, I guess, was in a place in his life where our friendship gave him a reason to explore and imagine his life in a different way. Before long, exactly what his wife warned us about, spending too much time catching up, turned into a mess a year later.

The more I think about it, the more I realize it was just the devil trying to mess me up again. Regardless, God was in control and nothing happened because I wasn't walking in the flesh. "This I say then, Walk in the Spirit, and ye shall not fulfill the lust of the flesh" (Galatians 5:1). I never had sexual urges when I was with him, and I never looked to him as anything other than a brother. In my mind, we were family and I was thankful that I had found someone I could relate

113

D.Nile Rivers

to. I tried to explain this to him but he didn't believe me. Needless-to-say, his wife was right, and he allowed his emotions to get the best of him even after I left and went back to my reality of a life.

We stayed in touch, which I later learned only fueled the fire. I just figured that he was going through a phase of infatuation and would get over it. I didn't see it coming. I was totally blindsided when he told me that he had expressed his feelings to his wife about me; feelings I never acknowledged. I couldn't believe it. I was irate! I should have known better, but I didn't.

I went back the following year for a function. Prior to my return, I contacted his wife and told her that I would be there and that we would have the opportunity to sit down and talk. She agreed with this, and we decided that we would get together during my stay. Being there again was very stressful for me. I wanted to be able to speak to my friend and share with him what had been going on in my life, but at the same time I didn't want to cause any problems for his wife.

She was cordial to me when we saw each other again and indicated that I was still welcome at her home, but I didn't feel comfortable going over there any more. I was still a little in shocked over what had happened. I still checked and re-checked myself to see if my actions were misleading. I checked my flesh to see if I had had sexual feelings towards him, and I knew I didn't. But, it wasn't about me. I thought I was doing a good thing by allowing him to share his feelings and relaying them to her because he wouldn't. I thought I was being helpful because I cared about them both, but I wasn't. Things would never be the same. Instead of feeling comfortable and at home, I felt ill at ease and like an intruder.

I dreaded going over to talk to her about what had happened. I didn't know where to start, especially since she had warned us that it would happen. I felt remorse because of what our friendship had caused. I never wanted to hurt her, and I told her that.

Once I explained my side of things to her, she told me that she didn't blame me for her husband's feelings, but she did hold me responsible for all the time we spent emailing and talking which aided to the end result. I understood this. She also told me that her husband had taken responsibility for how things turned out. As a result of everything, we came to the understanding that I would not talk to her husband unless it was to catch up once in a while. It wasn't what I wanted, but because of what had transpired, there was no way I was

Finding Mr. Right

going to be the cause of any more hurt.

We both agreed that her husband should be a part of the meeting, so we decided that the three of us would sit down and talk before I returned to the States.

When the three of us discussed what had happened, I made an attempt to explain what I felt and what he had shared with me about his feelings. I shared with her what made sense to me; that her husband was at a place in his life where he needed to be himself. He had lived the past twenty years with her and wasn't completely honest with her by not being "himself." Instead, he became someone else in order to be with her when he married her, and now he just wanted "to be." Then, unsuspecting me came along and I became the scapegoat or the answer to what he needed at that point in his life. We were able to communicate with each other, and it drew us close together. It was an exciting feeling, to be understood and accepted for who we were, instead of who people thought we were.

I tried to explain to her that it wasn't her fault that he pretended to be someone he was not, in order to be with her. I even told her that I had repeatedly told him that he needed to fess up to her with the truth. I told her that I was thankful that I was the one who came along and not someone of the world because I was walking in the Spirit, and, therefore, wouldn't give in to the flesh, which enabled her husband to share things that he needed to share with someone who wouldn't take advantage of the situation.

Whatever I learned from her husband during our talks, I shared with her in such a way as to let her know how he was feeling and what he was going through. He was aware of this the entire time because my desire was to help her understand him more. She wasn't receptive to what I tried to do. I couldn't blame her. She couldn't understand how I could know so much about her husband in one year, and she had been with him for twenty. I expressed to her that I cared about them both and that they were like family to me, which is why I was in the middle to begin with, but that didn't go over well either.

In the end, we got things out in the open. I was hurt because I lost a very good friend. She was hurt because she felt like I betrayed her after she had opened up her house to me and had treated me like family. I apologized to her for my part in anything I did to create the problem, and I was extremely angry with him for where he allowed things to go on his end.

115

D.Nile Rivers

To this date, I have kept my word. I rarely ever speak to him.

Chapter Eighteen

Mistaken Identity

One thing I learned from the experience with my *old time* friend was that whomever I got involved with again would have to be a good communicator. I realized that what made things so great between us was our ability to talk to each other. I hadn't realized before how great a need this was for me. I knew that being ignored and not being able to communicate in my relationships bothered me, but I never actually analyzed it to determine why it bothered me. Now I understood.

The relief and release associated with being able to talk and be heard was enlightening and uplifting because it felt like an unloading of sorts. It felt like I had held so much in for so long that once I had a listening ear, I couldn't talk fast enough to get all the years of silence out. I realized, for the first time in my life, that I had spent so much time being someone I was not in order to please others, that I had gotten to a point in my life where I was just tired and wanted to be myself.

I developed a huge appreciation for him that enabled me to bond with him in a way I'd never done with a man before. I truly believe that if we could have found the words to express this to those involved, the results might have been different. Of course, this probably wouldn't have changed his feelings towards me, but I believe that if he had been able to express himself to his wife the way he was able to express himself to me, she would have had the opportunity to appreciate the real him that was dying to come out. I tried to convince him to express all this to his wife, but he refused based on his belief that she wouldn't understand.

Once I realized my need for communication, I was able to

D.Nile Rivers

understand myself more. It was a great feeling, but I still had a lot to learn.

A couple weeks after the forty-day fast ended, I went to church, like I normally did on Wednesday nights, to counsel the teenage girls during Family Training Hour. It had been business as usual, but this night would be the beginning of a whole new chapter in my life.

At some point during the night, I left my class to retrieve something I had forgotten in my car. When I got to the hallway at the top of the stairs, Pastor stopped me and introduced me to a gentleman he was on his way downstairs with. This individual extended his hand to greet me. I extended my hand in return and immediately regretted it. He held my hand in such a vice grip that I'm sure he was able to see the discomfort I tried to hide on my face. I was used to shaking men's hands, but this was ridiculous. He gave me with the impression that he intentionally squeezed my hand to cause me pain. Based on his painful grip, I was unable to pay attention to his name and barely remembered anything after that other than Pastor mentioning something about him being a new counselor for the young men's group. I mumbled that it was nice to meet him and went out the door to the parking lot. I didn't give him a second thought.

Once church was over and we were on our way home, Trey couldn't stop talking about this new teacher they had. He said his name was "Mace." I remarked that it was a strange name, and Trey explained that it was his street name. He went on and on about this man like he was the next best thing to sliced bread, but I didn't want to discourage him by seeming uninterested in what he was saying. He was excited, and it showed because he couldn't wait for the following Wednesday to be back in church. Now, this caught my attention. Trey hated church. I practically had to drag him with me every time I went. With this in mind, my interests in this man were now peaked because he had captured my son's attention.

The following Sunday morning, I purposely sought this man out once church was dismissed. He was sitting in the back of the church by himself. The majority of the people had already headed out and those remaining were engaged in conversation, but not him. He just sat there in silence.

As I made my way to the back of the church, I didn't see anything spectacular about him that would make me take a second glance. He was extremely light-skinned. He was about six feet tall and he

118

Finding Mr. Right

appeared to be heavy set. It wasn't easy to determine if he was overweight and wore big clothes to cover it up, or if he just wore big clothing because he liked to feel comfortable. Either way, I didn't care. I wasn't looking for a man and was hoping God would honor that prayer for me to remain single.

When I finally reached him, he stood up. I said, "Mace. You're Mace, right?"

He firmly said, "Yes."

I told him that I wanted to meet him because he had made such an impression on my son. He looked perplexed. He stated that he wasn't sure who my son was. I looked around and pointed to Trey as he headed out the back of the church. He shook his head in recognition. I asked him about his name, and he explained what it meant, but it went in one ear and out the next because the vocabulary he used to explain the name were words I had never heard nor knew the meanings of. When he was finished, I excused myself and told him that it was nice to meet him.

That five or ten minute conversation left a lasting impression; try as I could, for the next few days, I couldn't get this man out of my mind. I replayed our conversation in my mind to see what it was that had transpired between us, and I found nothing. Aside from the slow way he spoke, as if he thought about every single word before he said it and the tone of his voice, there was nothing else that stood out to me.

He wasn't physically my type and, aside from that, I wasn't interested in being with anyone. So every time I thought of him, I rebuked the devil. I even prayed and asked God to remove him from my thoughts like I had done with the previous men since Manny had passed away. But for some reason, he was still in my mind, and I started having thoughts and a desire to see him again. Suddenly, Wednesday couldn't come soon enough, and I was just as excited as Trey about hearing this man speak again. The devil was up to his tricks again, but I wasn't aware until it was too late. There was a hole or a kink in my armor that I didn't know about, as a result of not having grieved over the loss of Manny, and the devil took that opportunity to attack. "Put on the whole armour of God, that ye may be able to stand against the wiles of the devil" (Ephesians 6:11).

Wednesday came, and I made sure I had on something nice to look at. I wasn't trying to be tempting, but I wanted to be noticed. Why? I didn't even know this man! When the kids and I arrived, Mace wasn't

D.Nile Rivers

there, and for a moment I was disappointed. When the time came for the kids to go to their various classes, he still wasn't there. I was just about to give up hope that he would come when I almost ran smack into him in the hallway. My heart skipped for joy because he was there. Why? I was still rebuking the devil, but not as strongly anymore. I mentioned something unintelligible to him; I'm sure, along with a greeting of some sort. He had on a bright red hat to match his bright red shirt and bright red backpack. Still, I didn't feel the physical attraction. I told him that I had to get downstairs, and we went our separate ways.

Well, that was all she wrote! My concentration was pretty much out the door for the rest of the night. I did what I could to find reasons to leave my class to go out to see him, even though I knew he was busy with the guys.

When I finally got the chance to break away from my class, I tried to walk by him as if I didn't notice him, but what I saw made me stop. Instead of teaching the young men, their former teacher was with them and Mace was with the little boys watching cartoons and watching over them. He didn't look happy and neither did the young men, who seemed very uninterested in what was being said to them. I stopped and asked him what happened, and he didn't want to talk about it. He said it was all right. I advised him to check with Pastor when he got the chance.

Once church was over, the young men couldn't wait to corner him and speak to him. Well, I couldn't wait either, but I played it cool. For some reason, I was intrigued by what he had to say. The devil was aware that my desires had changed from needing sex from a man to communication.

When he finally had a moment, I approached him, and as he spoke I stared at his mouth. Every now and then I would look at his eyes. He showed me some papers that he wanted to discuss with the young men and also allowed me to read a couple of his poems. I told him that I wrote poetry, as well.

As I read, it was nothing compared to what I normally read or anything I would write. The things he spoke of were extremely deep, and a few times I had to stop reading to ask him what a word meant so I could have a better understanding of what he was trying to say. When I was finished reading two of his poems, I had to go. The kids were getting impatient, but I really didn't want to leave. I wanted

Finding Mr. Right

more time to speak to him and get to know him.

I reluctantly went up the stairs. He mentioned that he was going to speak to Pastor and asked me if I would wait. I told him that I would, but after a few minutes had gone by, and there were only two or three cars left in the parking lot, I decided to go inside to see what was keeping him. As I entered the hallway leading to Pastor's office, I could hear them talking, and it didn't seem as if they were in any hurry to end their conversation. I decided to write my number on a piece of paper and give it to him so we could continue the conversation later on that night. I interrupted their conversation and said, "It doesn't seem like you two are in any hurry to leave, but I have to go. Here is my number, you can call me and we can continue our conversation if you want." He said, "I'm on my way out." By the time I got to my car, he was coming out of the church.

He smiled as he opened the paper I gave him. He retrieved his cell phone from his waist and said that it would be better if he just put the number in his phone right then. He smiled as he did this. Somehow, I think he discovered that I was just trying to make sure that he had my number.

I thought about him on the way home. I tried to pretend that I was present in mind as the kids spoke to me during the ride, but I was anywhere but present in the car with them. We hadn't had much of a conversation still at this point, but I couldn't get him out of my thoughts. I couldn't wait to get home and get the kids to bed so I could be available to talk. By the time he called, I was about to get in bed, but not ready to sleep.

We spoke until the sun came up. He got into reading his poetry, and I got so involved that I got my poetry, and we read to each other back and forth. We had poems with similar stories, but from different angles. My poems were mushy and nice; his were deep and rough. From the poetry we talked about anything and everything until I saw daylight poking through the clouds outside my bedroom window. Reluctantly, I told him I had to close my eyes for a little while before I went to work so I wouldn't be a complete mess.

After that night we talked every day and most times until the night was giving way to day. I didn't want anyone to know about him because I didn't want anyone to tell me anything I didn't want to hear. I didn't even tell my closest friend, Zoe.

There was something different about me. I wasn't necessarily

D.Nile Rivers

smiling more than usual because I was tired first of all, but I was accused of having a twinkle in my eye. It must have been the way the light hit my eye or something. I didn't know what they were talking about. All I knew is that I was being mentally stimulated. I had someone whom I could communicate with again, like my friend back home, and I was enjoying it. But this was different. Subconsciously I wondered if this was the man God intended for me. The more time I spent with him, the more I prayed and asked God. The problem arose when I prayed, but didn't wait for an answer.

By the end of the first week, I could hear a little birdie saying those three little words in my ear, "I love you." I wasn't about to say them and kept rebuking the feelings. At this point, we had spent time walking at the track, sitting on the bleachers for hours talking. We had been on the phone for hours talking, and the best part of all was that it wasn't sexual for me. For the first time in my life, it wasn't about physical attraction and I was enjoying it. I was still praying and asking God for guidance and to remove him if it wasn't His will, but he wasn't going anywhere.

Apparently, he had heard the same little birdie I had heard because by the end of the first week, he asked me if I felt like saying three words to him. I told him that I had felt like it, but that I wasn't going to say them. He said, "Do you see us walking down the aisle together?" I told him that I didn't know.

As time progressed, I kept asking and wondering if he was the one God intended for me. I went to my mentor and I asked him, "How do you know when it's the One?" He said a few things, but what stood out the most for me was when he said, "No matter what you do, you can't get that person out of your head."

I spoke to Pastor about it as well and asked him if he could imagine Mace and I together. He mentioned that he thought he was a nice guy. Well, I had to go to God because I just couldn't trust anyone else's opinion. I needed to know that this was God's will and not something that the devil was placing in my way to mess me up.

In the midst of reflecting one day, I was reminded about the forty-day fast and how one of the requests on the list we prayed for was for God to send saved, single men and women in the church. I also remembered a discussion Pastor and I had a few months after Manny passed away when he asked me if I thought I would ever marry again. I told him that I never wanted to marry again and that I just wanted to

Finding Mr. Right

remain single. He looked at me and said, "If it's God's will there is nothing you can do about it." I told him that I had prayed and asked God to just let me be alone. He said, "The man God has for you will be perfect for you. He will be everything you need in a man."

He instructed me to change my prayer from asking God to let me be alone to "God, have your way." He said that I should pray and be very specific in my request to him about what I wanted or needed. So I did. I thought I did.

Was Mace the man God had created for me? I wondered to myself. I had prayed for him to like to clean as a habit instead of a chore; for him to like to communicate; for him to be attentive and affectionate. I prayed for him to have patience and to love me for me. When I couldn't think of anything else, I simply said, "God, your will be done. Whomever you have for me, let me know beyond a doubt when I meet him, and let him know beyond a doubt that I am his." Little did I know the devil had heard my prayer as well regarding God's intended mate for me.

So far, he seemed to fit the requirements of some of the qualities I requested in my mate, but to look at him, he wasn't someone I would have picked for myself. He wasn't my type. I didn't like men with stomachs that looked like they were pregnant. He looked like he had a belly, but I couldn't really tell because he wore clothes that looked at least two sizes too big. He wore sweatpants all the time with button down shirt over t-shirts and always complimented his outfit with a baseball cap. He was extremely quiet to the point where it seemed eerie, and he had a look about him that made him seem scary and unapproachable. Just based on all this, I wouldn't have given him a second thought. But I did.

What attracted me to him was his mind. Since I wasn't attracted to him physically, I didn't spend a lot of time checking him out because if I did, then I wouldn't want to be with him. But to speak to him was a different story.

I'm sure if I had stopped speaking the majority of the time, he would have been more forthcoming with information about himself, but I was so caught up in the fact that I was actually speaking and someone was actually listening that it could wait. Mace was smart; what he was actually doing was taking in everything that I was saying and storing it in his memory bank. He often compared his memory to that of an elephant. It didn't matter if it was dirt that I'd done in the

D.Nile Rivers

past or the good that I'd done, his analytical mind was processing everything I said and, not only was he storing the information, he was creating an image of me based on my past and not who I was at the present time. I didn't know this at the time, but I found out soon enough.

When I finally did stop speaking, which was rarely, I would listen to Mace. He spoke proper English, which was strange because just to look at him you wouldn't think that he would speak the way in which he did. I enjoyed listening to him speak because he took the utmost care in choosing his words, and you could tell that whatever he had to say was deliberately said. I tucked this away in my memory bank. Other than for those reasons, to let the truth be told, I just liked watching his lips when he spoke. He had well-defined lips.

It didn't take long before I realized that the majority of the information being shared was from me. When I tried to get into his background, he simply said, "I'm a private person." I knew better than to press the issue and just concluded that when he was ready, he would open up. I had been patient this long so I could wait.

The first time I picked Mace up to come over to my house (he didn't have a car), he had me meet him at a corner near a car rental place. I found this odd, but based on his previous comment about being a private person, I let it slide. Having been a cop for six years, this should have caused red flags to go up, and they tried, but I squashed them. Trusting that God had sent my mate to me, I wasn't going to doubt.

I called Mace from my cell phone to let him know that I was at the corner waiting for him. As I waited, I called Sister Carol, a woman I knew from the church who had moved out of town. I told her about Mace and how we met at church. By the time Mace arrived at the car, I was still in the midst of my conversation, so I asked him if he wouldn't mind driving. He didn't seem to mind.

Since he didn't know where I lived, in between my phone conversation with Sister Carol, I gave him directions to the highway. Now, we were in a 1994 Nissan Maxima, which, regardless of how old, has a powerful engine. As Mace hit the highway and a stretch of road where I knew the troopers normally hid, I told him to slow down. Instead he said, "I got this." Well, no sooner had I warned him, than Mace flew by a trooper parked in a dark area on the side of the road, and as you can imagine, we got pulled over. I told Sister Carol that

Finding Mr. Right

we were being pulled over, and we both began to pray.

When the trooper walked up to the driver's side window, he asked for Mace's driver's license and the car registration. Mace handed him the registration and some other papers. I was still on the phone with Sister Carol. When the trooper finally came back, something wasn't right. I had to end my phone conversation and pay attention. Apparently Mace didn't have a license on him. He told the police officer that he had lost his license. Instead, he gave him his social security number. The trooper went back to his cruiser, and when he came back, he told Mace that they couldn't find any information on him. The trooper then turned his questions to me. He said, "Is this your car?"

I said, "Yes, officer. I was on the phone and asked him to drive."

Meanwhile I was praying that he would just let us go with a warning. The trooper had every right to arrest Mace, but by the grace of God, he simply told me to drive, and gave Mace a ticket for speeding. As I drove away, I looked at Mace who simply smirked and said, "Guess I can't use that name anymore." I didn't think it was funny. Flashing lights went off in my mind, but I shrugged them off.

When we finally arrived at my house, he said, "You let a complete stranger in your house." He was right. We had talked for hours on end, but I still didn't really know "who" he was; neither did the police. I offered to take him home, but I didn't feel like going back out and decided to see the night through and drop him off in the morning.

D.Nile Rivers

Chapter Nineteen

Doing My Own Thing

I didn't need anyone to tell me that there was something different about Mace. He definitely wasn't your *usual suspect*, I mean, man. Somehow, I was able to see beyond what he portrayed himself to be—mean and strange.

A street-wise thug is the best way I can think to describe the way he presented himself. He had a way of walking that seemed adopted instead of natural. I didn't know if it was done to appear cool, but I wasn't impressed.

Regardless of anyone else's opinion, however, he must not have been too bad because the boys at church couldn't wait to listen to him speak or have him around. Every Wednesday night they couldn't wait to get to church to listen to their new counselor.

Mace was able to relate to them because they spent the majority of their time in the streets, and since he was coming from the streets, he had something to say that they wanted to hear. According to him, he was able to break down the reality of money, cars, drugs, thugs, hustlers, etc., and offer them a different outlook on reality that made more sense. Whatever it was that he did with them seemed to work. They respected him and came out specifically to see him, my son included.

Though the youth were taking to Mace just fine, the grown-ups in the church weren't so accepting. Because Mace didn't speak much, he was a mystery, and that wasn't necessarily a good thing. People wanted to know who he was and what he was about. This became an issue to

126

Finding Mr. Right

the point where people actually went to Pastor and requested a background check be conducted on him. Mace wasn't pleased, and rightfully so, because I hadn't known of a background check being done on any one before. But I understood their concern. He really couldn't blame them because he purposely set out to appear strange and eerie to people. They were simply receiving him the way he wanted to be received, strangely.

"Ye shall know them by their fruits. Do men gather grapes of thorns, or figs of thistles?" (Matthew 7:16)

Because Mace refused to trust people and let them in, he remained a mystery, which only caused unnecessary problems. I'm sure he had his reasons.

If I went to visit a friend or family member, he deliberately remained in the car no matter how much I pleaded with him to meet them. He wouldn't budge. He didn't see anything wrong with his behavior. It didn't matter to him that people found his behavior weird. I'm not one to try to please people either, but this type of behavior was definitely strange. I later learned it's just his temperament; he prefers to limit who he socializes with and when.

It wasn't uncommon for us to go somewhere and for him to just stay in the car. We went to New York one day and I decided to visit Manny's sister while I was there. I begged him to meet her and her family. He refused. Instead, he stayed in the car while I visited, which made me feel awkward and hurried because I didn't feel right having him stay in the car for hours on end. His explanation: it was Manny's, family not his.

This happened enough times that I simply preferred for him not to go anywhere with me because I didn't like having to explain his behavior. If we did go somewhere together, I simply told people that he was anti-social.

The true test of his abnormal behavior was coming: Memorial Day weekend. It was that time of year when my siblings and I got together to hang out, catch up on each other's lives, and have a good time. This year, Mom was actually in the U.S. and would be there as well. This would be my opportunity to introduce Mace to the entire family. He already knew my son, Trey and my daughter, Morgan.

Of course, he didn't want to go because he didn't like being around

D.Nile Rivers

people much, but after much coercion, he decided to go. I think it was mainly to shut me up, but I can't say for certain.

I didn't really know what to expect for a reaction from my siblings, and it really didn't matter. I was just thankful he agreed to go.

At this point in our relationship, things were still fairly new, but at the same time it felt as if we'd known each other for years. All the talking we'd done, which had led to many sleepless nights conversing on the phone or walking around the track at the college, gave us the opportunity to communicate more than I had done in my previous relationships as a whole. It was thrilling and uplifting to be able to just talk about anything and everything. To me, it was a welcome change.

By the time Memorial Day rolled around, I felt very close to Mace; closer than I'd ever been within a three-week period of time with any man I'd met before. Sure, I had been close to men before, but it wasn't the same. This wasn't a physical thing; it was a mental thing. I wasn't even thinking about sex because I knew that it wasn't what I wanted. I had been celibate long enough not to think about sex like I used to.

We all (my three sisters and two brothers, their children, my uncle and Mom) went to a park to enjoy the day. The park was located somewhere in Pennsylvania near a beach. It also had a park area for the kids to hang out. It was a nice area, but when Mace and I went down by the water, there was decaying fish along the water close to the shore. The smell was horrid, but I seemed to be the only one totally offended by it. Was it a sign? Was God trying to tell me something? If He was, I didn't get it.

Even with this slight eye sore, there were still people in the water, around the water, hanging out in the sand, on the shore, etc. I didn't know about them, but my kids weren't going in that water.

As much as I wanted to spend time with my family who I hadn't seen all year, I wanted some alone time with Mace. We hung out at the picnic area with everyone for a while and then walked back down to the beach. We walked along the shore as we scouted out and were alarmed at the amount of dead fish. Surely there had to be something wrong with the water? We eventually climbed up to a mountainous rock formation, after stepping over small piles of debris and dead fish. It was worth it, though. The view and the peace and quiet we had there were our reward. I just wanted more time to talk.

Mace sat on the highest rock while I sat in front of him, between his legs, facing the water. As we talked we held hands or played with

Finding Mr. Right

each other's fingers. Now and then I would lean my head back against his chest and just enjoy being with him. Though I knew we weren't being very social, especially since we hadn't driven all this way to be alone, I tried not to let it bother me, but I knew we couldn't stay in our own little world for too long.

We eventually agreed that we had been gone long enough and walked back to the picnic area. But before we left the shore, we stopped for a brief moment (it felt like time stopped), and just hugged each other. It felt so safe, so warm, so inviting—sounds like temptation doesn't it? I didn't want to let go, but we did because some of the kids had found their way to us and ruined the moment. But that's how things were with Mace: being with him made me feel at home, as if we were a part of each other.

By the time we got back to where everyone was, it was time to eat, and rightfully so. Without even a second thought, I got Mace a plate and served him. It was totally out of character for me because I wasn't used to serving a man. It just wasn't something I would have done back in the day. A lot of the food was foreign to Mace so I had to explain what everything was as he ate. It didn't matter what it was. Everything must have tasted pretty good because, before long, there was nothing left on his plate. He had seconds on the Roti (it's a sort of tortilla shell with curry chicken and potatoes in it) and the mixed rice with codfish.

When he was finished, I spent a little more time with him, hugging him from time to time while he caressed my back. I'm mentioning this because Mom felt the need to say, "Mace seems to be very familiar with your body." I didn't want to read into what she said, but I knew where she was going with her thoughts. I'm sure she thought that Mace and I were sleeping with each other, but we weren't. I later thought that the reason Mace seemed so familiar with my body was because I was his "rib" and of course, he had to be familiar with his own body!

Once our bellies were full, I decided to relax on a blanket we had laid out on the grass. My sisters decided to join me as we watched the guys play soccer. Mace had a point to prove, and instead of taking it easy, ended up injuring his Achilles' tendon and was unable to walk without hopping on one foot. He did his best to pretend he was all right, but it was just a matter of time before he was in such agony that he couldn't hide it.

D.Nile Rivers

By the time we decided to call it a day, Mace was in severe pain and had to be escorted by my brothers to the car, which I had to pull up as far as I could on the grass to make the distance shorter for him to travel. He still did his best to act macho, but I knew better.

We said our farewells and headed in various directions to our homes. When we got on the highway, Mace had an asthma attack that lasted the duration of the four and a half hour trip home. I didn't know what to do and he refused to go to the hospital. He kept telling me that he was okay, but it was obvious to me that he wasn't. It was then that he decided to tell me that he was allergic to grass. He knew this, but still decided that he would spend his afternoon playing soccer and kicking up the grass trying to impress everyone with his moves. I didn't think this had been a wise decision on his part. He told me that he would be fine, and I did my best not to make him talk the rest of the way home.

I still didn't know what to do when we got to my house, where he would stay for the night. I did the best I could to make him feel comfortable on the couch, by wrapping ice around his Achilles tendon and whatever else I could. I was very concerned about his breathing and decided to spend the night on the floor while he slept on the couch beside me. I didn't get much sleep because I kept checking to make sure he was breathing throughout the night.

By morning Mace's breathing had been restored to normal and he was able to talk freely. He mentioned that in order for him to get past his reaction to grass that the best thing for him to do was to face it head on. I didn't agree with this concept, but apparently this was the way he had dealt with other things in the past and it must have worked. As for his Achilles tendon, it was still causing him a lot of pain and preventing him from walking properly. I was able to get a used crutch for him to use later on that day, but he decided not to use it.

Finding Mr. Right

Chapter Twenty

Tunnel Vision

Mace and I continued to meet at the track and talked on the phone daily. We also did the movie thing and went out to eat from time to time.

On one occasion, I called him and asked him if I would be seeing him later on that night. He mentioned that he didn't think he would be coming over and that was not the response I wanted to hear. I tried to pretend like it wasn't a big deal, but as the conversation went on, my blood started bubbling, and eventually, I had something to say about his decision. The longer he spoke and I remained silent and gave him short answers, the more he got the hint that I wasn't pleased with his decision. I eventually told him how I felt. I said, "You only want to see me when it's convenient for you. What about when I want to see you?"

Well, that didn't go over very well, but the longer we stayed on the phone, the more I was able to persuade him to come over. Unfortunately, I had to twist his arm to come over and by the time I picked him up he wasn't too pleased with me. He decided to demonstrate his displeasure by punishing me with his silence.

He knew that this was something that didn't sit well with me. I had practically told him everything about me, to include the things that I didn't like, and he knew that being ignored was one of them. This was one of those instances where he used information I had given him as ammunition against me. Note to self.

Mace knew that in my previous relationship with Manny, that there were times when Manny would pass me by without speaking, even though I hadn't done anything wrong. Mace knew this was an issue

131

D.Nile Rivers

with me and used it as a means of punishing me. So, basically, I got exactly what he thought I deserved as a result of the tantrum I had used to persuade him to come over. In other words, Mace came over to appease me, but he stayed to himself to prove a point. I got the point, but it didn't make things any better.

The ride back to his place the next day was pretty quiet. I didn't know where to start, but I wasn't about to leave things the way they were. I made a stop to get something to drink and while I did, I picked up something for him as well. When I got back into the car, I gave him a single red rose and told him that I was sorry for my behavior.

After a few more minutes of driving, Mace decided to speak. Instead of getting past the night before or the tantrum, he decided to keep the fire burning. I would later learn that he lived his life by keeping fires ablaze.

Without warning, Mace said, "You gave me a rose. Roses have thorns. Thorns draw blood." I listened in disbelief.

He continued, "Roses have a shelf life of about two weeks." Well, he didn't need to say anything else. I pulled the car over into a parking lot not too far from his corner. I still didn't know where he lived. I couldn't believe that he took my gesture and something as beautiful as a rose and made it into something so ugly. This wouldn't be the last time he would do this.

I pulled away from that parking lot bewildered. Flags kept going up, but I kept pushing them down. In my mind I kept thinking that he was the *One,* and though he might have some issues, I was willing to deal with them because of who I believed him to be.

Later on that night, Mace called me to tell me that he didn't want to see me anymore. He really didn't have a good reason other than he felt we should end it. Well, at that point I was in love with him, and I wasn't willing to accept his decision. Could this have been my way out? Was this God giving me a sign? If He was, I didn't receive it that way.

After speaking to Mace for a while on the phone, I decided to go see him. He wasn't sounding too good. At this point, I had gotten to know his moods and his tones enough to know when something just wasn't right with him. He still didn't share his feelings much or let me in, but I could tell when there was a shift in him.

I didn't tell him that I was driving out to see him. I just kept him on the phone until I got to the track. At first, I didn't see his mother's

132

Finding Mr. Right

van, his means of transportation. He wasn't expecting me, so I just asked him where he was. He knew my car so he saw me when I pulled up. We had a certain parking lot that we used when we went to the track and apparently that is where he was, but I didn't see him.

He reluctantly told me where he was and got out of the van to meet me. We sat on a nearby picnic table. I tried to talk to him, but I realized that silence was the better thing to do.

Every now and then he spoke, but it was like pulling teeth. He had already made it clear that he didn't trust people, and less so, women. He had no problem telling me, "All women are Eve." I didn't agree, but kept it to myself. He said that he preferred dealing with children because they were honest.

The minutes ticked by, and I played with the grass with my feet as I waited for him to release some steam. It was slow going, but little by little he let certain things out. It was hard for him or maybe he just wanted it to be hard for him, because, to me, it was really simple. Just open your mouth and speak!

I was reminded of myself. He reminded me of a time when I wanted to speak and couldn't; when I spoke, but my lips didn't actually move. When I used to will the person in front of me to hear what my mouth wasn't saying. So I understood what he was going through to some extent. My silence, on the other hand, wasn't to shut people out because I didn't trust them. My silence was a defense mechanism brought on because of my childhood fears. Mace, on the other hand, did it as a means of security.

From the bits and pieces of things that Mace said, remember this is a man who chose his words very carefully and only said what he meant, I was able to understand that he was dealing with past issues that he refused to let go.

"Brethren, I count not myself to have apprehended: but this one thing I do, forgetting those things which are behind, and reaching forth unto those things which are before."
(Philippians 3:13)

Mace had a lot of pent up anger over things that happened in his past that he wouldn't let go. I didn't understand why he wouldn't just let things go, especially since he was saved and knew the Bible and what it said about anger.

D.Nile Rivers

"But now ye also put off all these; anger, wrath, malice, blasphemy, filthy communication out of your mouth." (Colossians 3:8)

Time passed by quickly, and it was getting late. I had to work in the morning and the late nights of staying up with Mace were beginning to take their toll on me.

Mace walked me over to my car, about 25 feet from where we were, but he wasn't ready for me to leave. I wasn't ready to leave either. He leaned his back against the driver's side door, hands in his pocket, the brim of his hat tilted down over his glasses so you could barely see his eyes, with his head bent down. I stood in front of him not saying anything. And since I didn't know what to say, I simply stepped closer to him and held him. I slipped my arms through his and just held him. I tried to convince him that he could talk to me; that it was all right. We stayed like that for a long time without either of us saying a word. I just wanted him to know that I was there for him.

When he finally spoke, he said, "I don't like to talk about my past. I'm a private person." He said, "Trusting people in my past is what got me where I am today, left without anything."

He reiterated that he didn't trust people. I simply listened. His anger was very apparent when he spoke. I could feel it just by holding him. I wished that I could take the anger away. It reminded me of a time when I used to pray and ask God to allow me to feel other people's pain. I wanted to help bear people's pain so they didn't have to go through it alone. It worked. Over the years, I have been able to feel people's pain. Funny, I had forgotten that I had asked for that ability.

In the past, there were times when all of a sudden I would cry uncontrollably, and there was nothing wrong with me. But then I would look around and see someone crying or I would call someone close to me and would understand. I didn't mind it at first because I knew how to take what I felt and give it to God in prayer. But I didn't always remember this, and there were times when I would take on someone else's pain or grief, and it stayed with me. Because I didn't give it up to God, it weighed me down, and I couldn't deal with it. Rightfully so; it wasn't mine to deal with. I was hardly able to deal with my own issues, let alone someone else's. Needless-to-say, somewhere along the way, I learned to shut that part of me off.

Finding Mr. Right

I was feeling Mace's anger, and it was deeper than anything I had ever experienced. All I could do was pray. I didn't know what else to do. It was a scary feeling, and I didn't want it to remain with me. It was clear to me that Mace's issues were intense and deep-rooted, and there was nothing I could do for him but to pray.

By the time Mace was through sharing some of his thoughts with me, he decided that it really was late and that I should get home. I told him that I wouldn't say anything to anyone about what he shared. I thanked him for sharing because it gave me a better understanding of who he was and what he'd been through. It also gave me a better understanding of what to pray about. We said our goodbyes; he tucked me in the car and sent me on my way. We spoke on the phone until I made it safely home, and we said goodnight.

Chapter Twenty-One

Dr. Jeckle and Mr. Hyde

People at church slowly became aware of the relationship Mace and I had. Some people were all right with it while, others thought it was too soon after Manny's passing to get involved. As far as I was concerned, I would always miss Manny; nothing was going to change that—not years or anyone else.

In my mind, I felt that I was ready to move on. I felt I could never get rid of the feeling of missing him, so I might as well get used to it, and that's exactly what I did. But did I? Had I really gotten used to being all right with missing Manny? I thought I had.

What I didn't realize was that I was using Mace to try and fill the same void I had been trying to fill with each man I got involved with. The devil knew this and because I had been spending so much time talking to Mace, I convinced myself that God was in our midst when in reality it was the devil, trying to distract my purpose. As a result, instead of listening and being obedient, I listened to what I wanted to hear and welcomed adversity with open arms.

I heard a minister on television say, "You never marry who you think you are going to marry. It's not usually someone you would normally choose." I took all of this into consideration, along with my unanswered prayers for Mace to be removed from my life, and concluded that he must be the *One*.

I thought back on my prayer to God regarding my mate. I recalled asking Him to make it clear to me and to him that we were meant to be together. Well, based on what we both knew and felt, I decided he was it.

Regardless of what I felt, Trey wasn't having it. The moment Mace

Finding Mr. Right

and I became an item, Trey changed. I didn't recognize him any more. He was jealous and angry at the same time. He even went so far as to say, "If I want to break you two up, I can." I shrugged his comment off, but would later be reminded.

When I had enough of Trey's disrespectful behavior, Mace and I sat him down and tried to find out what was bothering him. He said, "Mace told me that he was here for me when we first met, and now he spends all his time with you." Clearly, he was jealous.

He also said, "I am the man of the house, and I will never accept him as the man of the house." I tried to explain to Trey that *I* was tired of being the man of the house. Even in my previous marriages, I was always the man. I told him that I was tired of having to be in charge all the time, and that I was ready to give that over to someone else. Yes, I had told Trey that he was "the man" as he grew up, but he was the only man at the time. I guess I didn't make that clear enough throughout the years.

Trey's disrespect escalated and Mace only made it worse. Mace felt it was his duty to bring out the worst in him.

Mace came to visit and never left. He said that the Holy Spirit told him, "Dwell with her in understanding." I had a problem with this, but he didn't care. I guess he didn't mind sleeping on the couch, which didn't last long either. Eventually, he decided that he wasn't sleeping on the couch. Well, when he slept in the bed, I decided to sleep in the couch. I told him that it wasn't right in the sight of God; regardless of whether or not we felt we were "it" for each other. He went through the same speech I heard other men before him say, "Well, you know that in the sight of God, all we have to do is declare our love for each other like back in the Old Testament days, etc." I wasn't hearing that. But Mace didn't need me to remind him of what the Bible said. He was very well versed in the Scriptures and their meanings. So much so that he had a tendency to make me feel as if I didn't know anything and had me second-guessing myself.

"The thief cometh not, but for to steal, and to kill, and to destroy…" (John 10:10)

I didn't force the issue of him staying, as long as he did the right thing. Clearly I wasn't thinking straight. Besides, he wasn't the type of person you told what to do. He did what he wanted and when he

D.Nile Rivers

wanted. I had opened up Pandora's Box and didn't know how to close it. I just kept praying.

While drilling at Devens one weekend, I got a call from Lenny, telling me that the police were at my house. He said that Morgan had called the police because Trey and Mace were going at it. I immediately told my supervisor that I had to leave and was released to go home.

By the time I got home, Trey and Morgan had left the house with Lenny. From what Mace said, he didn't do anything other than try to restrain Trey from hitting him. According to Trey, when I spoke to him, Mace instigated the whole thing. At the time I believed Mace, and Trey's disappointment in me was obvious.

On another occasion, Trey felt the need to disrespect me, and as a result, I made him do push-ups, which was his form of punishment over the years. But as I disciplined him, Mace felt the need to intercede, and made things worse. He antagonized Trey and heckled him about thinking he was the man. Trey eventually got up off the floor, after Mace had gotten on the floor to do push ups in front of Trey's face, and walked away.

Wherever Trey went, Mace also went, asking him, "So you think you tough." You think you the man?"

Trey kept saying, "Leave me alone." I did what I could to defuse the situation, but to no avail. I was eventually able to get Mace to stop.

I couldn't believe the disrespect Trey displayed. I couldn't really blame him, but I had never seen him show so much disrespect for a person in my life. Ever since Trey had turned sixteen, he had become different. I didn't know what happened to change his personality, but instead of listening to me and doing what I asked him to do, he had become more and more disrespectful. Now was no exception. It didn't matter what I said to him, he wasn't listening. Mace was clearly wrong for what he did, but he couldn't see it. Flags!

Another time, Lenny came over to the house just as Mace and I were on our way out the back door to go for a walk. As we walked from the back of the house towards the front sidewalk, we saw Lenny coming out the front door of the house. I didn't know he was even there. He bellowed to me, "I need to talk to you."

Who told him to say that, and especially in front of Mace? I didn't have a problem dealing with Lenny because I'd done it for years, but Mace had a thing for people who tried to make him look bad, whether

Finding Mr. Right

intentionally or not. In his mind, Lenny was being disrespectful: first of all, for going inside the house knowing that Mace now stayed there, and second, for talking to me like that in front of him.

I immediately started praying because I was aware of Mace's temper. Mace stepped around me and got in Lenny's face. He was so close that I knew he could tell whether Lenny's pores were open or closed.

Mace appeared calm, but I had come to know that he was extremely dangerous. He kept telling Lenny to back down when he was clearly wrong for going in Lenny's face. He tried a few times to get Lenny to hit him, but Lenny simply told him that it wasn't worth it. In the meantime, I kept trying to talk to Mace, who wasn't listening. So I prayed.

Mace's behavior allowed me to see him in action and to confirm what Trey had said, that he instigated the incident they had previously. I had to apologize to Trey for not believing him. "Therefore whatsoever ye have spoken in the darkness shall be heard in the light… (Luke 12:3)."

When I mentioned to Mace that he didn't have to do what he did, he said, "No one is going to punk me."

I said, "You got in his face. You didn't have to push up on him like that."

We obviously weren't going to agree on this, and since I didn't want an argument with him, I kept quiet after that. More flags!

The incidents just kept coming. There would be calm for a while and then hell would seem to break loose for the simplest of reasons.

Trey kept on being disrespectful because Mace was still around. Apparently Mace was a whole different person when I wasn't home. Trey didn't bother telling me anything after that, probably because I didn't believe him that one time.

One day Trey said something to me that Mace perceived as disrespectful. I didn't think anything of what Trey said, but Mace got so mad that he made an attempt to go after Trey who had no idea and had already gone upstairs. I immediately went to the door leading to upstairs and shut it. I also immediately started to pray and ask God for help because I knew that there was no way I could hold him back. He weighed a hundred pounds more than I did.

As I tried to calm Mace down, standing by the door leading upstairs, I prayed. I told him, "You are not going upstairs after my son,

139

D.Nile Rivers

in the name of Jesus!" As we stood there, Mace started to rock back and forth, something he did when the rage began to rise inside him. His face started to twitch, and he began to grind his teeth, which I could hear clearly on the outside of his head. His eyes got really beady looking, and I knew that if God didn't intercede NOW...

He eventually calmed down, and that was the end of that. Warning flags, but I still didn't do anything.

Mace stayed, "dwelling with us in understanding." In my mind, I kept thinking that we were supposed to be together and that God would work things out. That was the only thing that kept me with this man, my belief that it was God's will.

Chapter Twenty-Two

Wolf in Sheep's Clothing

"Beware of false prophets, which come to you in sheep's
clothing, but inwardly they are ravening wolves."
(Matthew 7:15)

In between the scary moments of dealing with Mace, he was really
a nice guy. I realized he had deep-rooted issues, but I wasn't afraid. I
still thought I was supposed to be in his life and that God would work
it out for His good.

We would have some really great moments, and then he would just
flip the script. For example, I took Mace to drill with me one day
during one of my make-up training days. The day started off great.
We talked from time to time, but for the majority of the day Mace
stayed in the break room writing his poetry (something he spent
numerous hours doing).

Throughout the day I would take a break from working and hang
out with him for a little while. I went to see him at some point during
the day and found that his mood had changed. One minute I was
sitting on the table in front of him and the next minute he had his face
in my chest crying. All I could do was pray. And of course, he didn't
want to share what was bothering him. When he calmed down, I went
back to work and continued to pray.

This was my last month at drill. I had finally reached my goal of
twenty years and could retire. But I didn't really want to retire. I
wanted to have achieved more rank prior to retiring, but I didn't
because I had stopped trying. I had gotten so frustrated with being
under-utilized that I just didn't have the desire to be there, even when

D.Nile Rivers

I was there.

I wanted to stay in, but become an officer. I mentioned this to Mace who calmly said, "You're not staying in. If you stay in I'll break both your legs." He said that he didn't want me to be shipped overseas to war, and since I couldn't get pregnant due to tubal ligation after Morgan was born, he said the only way he could keep me from going was if I was injured. He said all this very calmly and without missing a beat. I knew that he was serious, but I wasn't afraid of him. Still, I knew he was very capable of doing what he said. And still I prayed.

It was times like these when I just didn't get it. I mean, I knew what the Bible said about being a new creature in Christ once you got saved. I knew that certain things Mace did and said didn't line up with the Bible. But I kept thinking, "He is the *One* God intended me to be with." So I trusted that God would work out whatever needed to be done in him.

In the meantime, I stayed with him because I just knew...even with his mood swings and his unpredictability, there were moments when he spoke, and I just *knew* it was the Holy Spirit in him. Then there were times when he spoke, and I knew it wasn't. I could see the battle between the flesh and spirit within him.

> "For we wrestle not against flesh and blood, but against
> principalities, against powers, against the rulers of the
> darkness of this world, against spiritual wickedness in high
> places." (Ephesians 6:12)

His fight was moment by moment; unlike some of us whose fight comes and goes. It was a fight no one could understand unless dealing with him in the capacity in which I was dealing with him in. But I wasn't afraid. I continued to pray. I prayed more than I ever did in my entire life.

Not only did I stay, but during one of the better moments earlier in the relationship, Mace and I decided that we would get married. I knew he had some serious defects, but I wasn't worried because I just knew God would work out His will in Mace. Or would he?

Mace told Pastor that we were going to get married. Pastor told him that we should wait. When I spoke to Pastor about it, he also told me that we should wait. Every one I told in the family said that I shouldn't do it. My girlfriend at work told me that I shouldn't do it.

142

Finding Mr. Right

My mentor said indirectly in Bible study one night, "Don't be in a rush to get married." Did I know he was speaking to me? More than likely. Did he personally come out and tell me not to get married? No. He wasn't the type of person that did that. Sometimes he just gave you a word and it was up to you to do what you wanted to do with it.

Up until this point, ever since Manny had passed away, my mentor and Pastor were there for me. They called me daily and I was in church at least four times a week. I surrounded myself with people from the church. They were my extended family and very present help in a time of need.

Talking about my decision to marry Mace wasn't an option. I knew he was the *One*. It didn't matter that when September rolled around we would only have known each other for five months. I justified it by saying, "It doesn't matter how long you know a person because you can never really know them." I based this on what had transpired between Manny and I. He had been with someone else the same three years he and I were building a relationship together. The whole time I had no clue that he was seeing someone else. I trusted him and had no reason not to. When I found out that we were living a lie, that I had married him based on a lie, it proved to me that you just never really knew a person.

With that in mind, I figured that I would just be with Mace and learn as I went. It wasn't as if he was holding back on the ugly side of him. At least that wasn't a secret. I had seen it and had dealt with it in prayer and figured that I trusted God and believed that Mace was it.

But something happened that changed my mind about getting married. It didn't have anything to do with anything anyone said, but it finally registered one day with something that Mace did.

I was in bed one night and about to call it a day when Mace came in to speak to me about something. He and I disagreed on something that was said, and he decided to walk away upset. As he turned to walk away, I tried to reach for his shirt. I barely caught it as I said, "Wait, let's talk about it." At the same time, Mace did a defensive maneuver (he is a five degree black belt) with his hand that caught my hand and hurt me.

I was caught off guard because I didn't know what I had done to deserve that, but it really wasn't so much what I had done, but what he thought I had done. In his mind, he thought I was being aggressive, but there wasn't anything in my mind geared towards aggression. I

143

D.Nile Rivers

tried to explain this to him, but he was beyond the point of listening.

From that moment, I realized that Mace was the type of man who didn't have a problem physically hurting a woman. My years as a police officer dealing with domestic violence issues came rushing back to me. Everything I'd learned reminded me that once a man put his hands on you, he would continue to do so.

I suggested to him the next day that we should postpone the wedding. With that, I told Pastor that I had postponed the wedding, as well as anybody else who knew.

Mace didn't say much about what happened, and he didn't feel like he should leave either. Things went back to business as usual, and life went on. My awareness was up now. I wasn't ignoring the flags any more.

Chapter Twenty-Three

Hook, Line, and Sinker

Life went on and we encountered speed bumps along the way. As they came, I prayed and kept on going. God had kept me thus far and continued to answer my prayers.

When September 10th, 2004 rolled around (two days before the wedding had been scheduled), I called Mace's family in New Jersey to make sure everything was all set with them knowing that I had cancelled the wedding. Well, to my surprise, they had no idea what I was talking about. They had already gotten the food for the wedding, the hall, the church, etc. I was mortified. I told them that I had cancelled the wedding a while ago and had told Mace to tell them. He never told them. I apologized for their inconvenience for all they had done. When I hung up the phone I immediately called Mace. He was off somewhere in one of his moods for whatever reason this time.

I was upset, and I shared this with him. I asked him, "Why didn't you tell your family that the wedding was cancelled?" He said, "You cancelled the wedding; you should have told them yourself." I couldn't believe my ears.

I called Pastor to ask him what to do, and he couldn't talk, but said that he would call me back. I prayed. I didn't know what to do. I knew he was the *One*, but there were things God needed to work out.

I stayed in bed praying and wondering what to do. Hours went by and I still hadn't heard from Pastor. I called him again, and he said that he would call me back. I never got to tell him what the problem was.

D.Nile Rivers

In between waiting on him and praying for an answer, Mace's grandmother called me. She was very upset, and by the time I was finished talking to her, I had decided that I would go through with the wedding. Dumb move.

I got out of bed and went to get my hair done at the last minute. I told him of the change in plans and he met me at the hairdresser's place. We talked briefly and I gave him money to buy something to wear for the wedding.

The next day, I went to the mall with Morgan to find a dress. We picked out a black dress (I was never the traditional bride) for me and we decided on a white dress for Morgan. When we were through, we all left for New Jersey. I know, doomed from the start.

I was extremely afraid, and it was really strange because I am not the type of person to be afraid of anything. But I was very afraid that I was doing the wrong thing. I hadn't heard from God, and I didn't want to make a mistake. Then why did I go through with it?

The next day, on the way to the church, I was afraid. When I got to the church, I was so afraid I didn't want to walk down the aisle. I had been married twice before, and I never felt as afraid as I did at that moment. If I knew then what I know now! The bait of Satan.

As I waited with Mace's grandmother in the foyer of the church, I paced. I kept telling his grandmother that I was afraid. His aunt should never have left me with her. Maybe if his aunt had stayed with me instead of his grandmother, I might have talked to her and she might have understood my fear.

I did walk down the aisle, and I did make a vow before God to be his wife.

Once the ceremony was done, we went back to his aunt's place and to the place they had set up for the reception. The only people at the wedding were his sister and her boyfriend, his stepfather, his uncle, aunt, grandmother and Morgan.

I could sense a change in Mace's mood at the reception. He said that he had a hunger headache and hoped it would go away once he had something to eat. We mingled and hung out for a little while until it was time to leave.

From that day on, all hell broke loose. For some reason we couldn't communicate without there being miscommunication or someone saying the wrong thing. I didn't understand. If there was nothing else we had, we had the ability to communicate with each

Finding Mr. Right

other because it was all we did. Not any more! All I could do was pray.

I continued to go to church and Pastor was not too happy that I had gone through with the wedding. I tried to explain to him that I had tried to reach him to tell him what happened, but it didn't matter because I should have stuck to my decision. I knew Pastor was disappointed in me, but he told me that he loved me, even though I hadn't listened. He mentioned that he wanted to announce to the church that we had gotten married, but I advised him not to.

My mentor wasn't pleased either; neither was his wife who loved me dearly. She mentioned that she was hurt because I hadn't told her that I was going to do it. I tried to explain to her that at first I wasn't and that it was a last minute thing for me. She asked me if I was happy, and I told her that I was—at the time.

I continued to go to church, but Pastor didn't call me like he used to. My mentor didn't call either. I knew it was because I hadn't listened and probably more so because they realized that I was going to do what I wanted anyway.

Things didn't change much because Mace had already been living in the house, whether I wanted him to or not. The only difference was that we were legally married. We still went to church and life went on as usual, with Mace's mood swings.

By November, things between Mace and Trey had gotten to the point where I couldn't take it any more and I asked Mace to leave. He wasn't pleased that I had chosen Trey over him. Regardless of Trey's disrespect, he was my flesh and blood.

Unfortunately, when December rolled around, Trey's behavior hadn't changed. When I confronted him about a pocket knife I found on his bed one day, he and I got into an argument. We were in the kitchen when I threatened to hit him with a pot cover in the dish tray as he walked away from me. He ignored me and went upstairs to his room. I followed him upstairs to his room to talk to him. I tried talking to him, but he refused to listen. When I went to hit him, he held my hands down. I tried to bite him so he would let me go. When he let me go, I told him that I wasn't going to put up with his disrespect.

He said, "I'm out of here."

"Bye", I said. I wasn't going to put up with the disrespect another minute.

147

D.Nile Rivers

I decided to help him with his stuff as he started to pack. I grabbed a couple of shoe boxes and told him I was taking them downstairs. Trey got mad and blocked the doorway leading out of Morgan's bedroom.

He said, "I bought those with my own money."

I responded, "I'm just helping you bring them downstairs." Trey knocked the boxes out of my hand and down the stairs. I looked at him in shock. I didn't know this side of Trey. He was out of control. I went downstairs and called 911. I told him that I wasn't putting up with his nonsense. When the police arrived, I told them what had happened. They asked me, "What do you want us to do?" I told them that he needed to leave. When they asked Trey what he wanted to do, he told them, "I'm not staying in this house." Before Trey left, he said, "I'll see you in hell." That hurt me more than he would ever know.

I watched Trey walk out of the house. It was hard letting him leave, but I had no control over him anymore. Trey ended up going to stay with Lenny for a while. When that didn't work out, he went to live with his aunt in Maryland, and then his uncle in Philadelphia. Trey was on a rampage. It didn't matter where he went, he didn't listen to anyone in authority. Ultimately, Trey got his GED and joined the Army.

Chapter Twenty-Four

One with the Enemy

It wasn't long before Mace and I, along with a sister and brother from the church (a group Pastor assembled to create events for the youth in the church) came up with a plan to have a Gospel rap concert in December. It was a great idea and we decided that since Mace had experience with promoting events and such, it would be an added plus. But Mace didn't want to work as a group. He wasn't used to working with people in this capacity and eventually took charge of the entire planning of things.

We didn't think it was a bad idea to let Mace take charge since he knew what he was doing. The problem arose when Mace became overwhelmed because he felt he had to do everything himself. Instead of telling us what to do, he took it upon himself to handle things, but got frustrated because of the red tape within the church and the lack of cash.

It really didn't have to be a problem, but it was. Mace fell back on his worldly experience as a promoter in order to deal with the event, which meant that flyers had to be made, tickets had to be made and sold, a venue had to be secured, and promotion of the event had to take place.

Because Mace hadn't been in the area a long time, I offered to use my contacts in the music and radio industry to help him promote the event. I didn't realize there were other people willing to help him out as well.

Earlier in the summer, I took my youth group to Six Flags for an outing. Heather, a mother of one of the girls in my group, got a little upset with me when she decided to volunteer her younger daughter, who was not in my class, to go along with us. There wasn't enough

D.Nile Rivers

room for all the girls to fit in the two vehicles that were going on the trip. As a result, Heather offered for me to take her vehicle, which was larger than mine, but I didn't want to. I asked her if she could just drop the extra girls off at the park and pick them up when it was time to leave. She didn't like this idea.

Prior to this incident, Heather and I spent time talking on the phone and getting to know each other. She was loud-mouthed, swore when she wanted to, and had an attitude that warned you not to mess with her. She didn't care what people said about her or what she said about people. She seemed to be an outcast at the church, but still, she knew just about everybody there.

I quickly learned that Heather had the 411 on just about everybody in the church. She seemed to know things that she shouldn't have known. I didn't know who her source was, but they were good.

I had the opportunity to be at the mall one day and ran into Heather. She was in the midst of disciplining one of her daughters in the shoe department of Sears. Heather didn't care who heard her, and she could actually have been heard clear to the other side of the mall if anyone was listening. As I observed, she reminded me of Mace. Her anger was so intense, and her words were so vile towards her twelve-year-old daughter that it made me feel for the girl. Her daughter was used to this, but it was something new to me. And as I took Heather in this new light, I made a mental note that she wasn't someone I needed to hang around with.

My concerns were confirmed by another sister in the church who was the present victim of Heather's wrath. Somehow I got in the middle of their mess, and one minute Heather was pulling me to hear her side and the next Jada was pulling me to hear hers. I didn't know which one to believe because they were both believable.

Jada tried to warn me about Heather, but I didn't listen. She tried to tell me about the kind of person that she was, a person who caused division, but I didn't see it. In the meantime I decided to get to know her based on who she presented herself to be and not based on her past. Big no-no.

I finally saw for myself what Jada had been talking about. Every time Heather saw Jada and I together, she would boldly come between us and start a conversation with me. I thought it was rude and would ask her to wait a minute, but she was very pushy. Jada would simply walk away. I didn't think anything of it, other than that Heather was

150

Finding Mr. Right

rude.

I introduced Heather to Mace one day, and she was surprised because she had no idea we had been an item. She gave us her stamp of approval and said that she wouldn't tell anyone. Now, I knew that Mace wasn't Heather's type because she was high maintenance and Mace didn't have a job, let alone any money to support her diamond habit, fancy truck repairs, or bankroll her wardrobe and that of her kids. So, I wasn't worried.

I saw Heather in the church parking lot one day holding Mace's hand, and I commented in a playful, but meaningful manner, "You holding his hand a little long aren't you?" Now this wouldn't have been a problem otherwise, but because she had a well-known reputation for messing with people's men, it became a problem.

After that day, Heather decided that she would make my life miserable because she didn't like the fact that I called her out like that. Whenever I saw her, I spoke to her, but she acted like she didn't know me. I mentioned this to Mace, but he said that she told him that *I* wasn't speaking to her. I looked at him as if he had two heads.

I said, "I have spoken to Heather on numerous occasions, and she acted as if she didn't know me."

He said, "Well that's not what she says."

In the midst of preparing for the upcoming December event, I did what I could and what I was allowed to do to help out. I was more than willing, but Mace decided that he didn't want to come to me for help. Instead, he accepted the services of, yes, none other than Heather, behind my back.

Mace decided to have the Gospel rappers come to the church as a pre-screening. The idea of Gospel rap wasn't readily accepted by the traditional people in the church and he wanted to give people the opportunity to hear what they actually had to say.

After the group performed, they left to promote the event at the radio station with Mace. I remained in the service, unaware that they had left. What I didn't know was that Mace left to go to the radio station, but Heather went as well.

Heather had taken it upon herself to offer her services and contacts to Mace even though she was not a part of the group putting on the event. Mace didn't see anything wrong with that. He had no idea what Heather was up to, but I did.

From that moment on, Heather did whatever she could to cause

D.Nile Rivers

problems in my life, and it worked to the point where I simply couldn't worship at that church any more. I tried to get past her as a distraction, but I eventually left.

I tried talking to Pastor about it, but got the usual "Everything will be all right" speech. Mace thought I was making things up, and every time I brought up her name I got yelled at or cursed out, so I learned not to bring it up.

The fact that Mace took Heather's side over anything I said was a problem for me. He didn't understand my irritation and frustration with her because he was either blind to her tricks or in cahoots with her to make my life miserable. The more I mentioned what she did, the worse the argument got. We got into it one day when I told him that he was always defending her. That day ended with me calling 911 because he threatened to burn my house down. If I didn't know any better....

Mace was definitely, "Like a box of chocolates; you never knew what you were going to get."

I had to take a trip to New York one weekend for a grant seminar. I asked Mace to go with me because he was from New York and I always got lost when I went by myself. Mace said he would go with me for the ride, but that he would stay in the car. The seminar was at least eight hours I told him, but he didn't care. I really didn't want him to go and spend all that time in the car, but he did.

During the seminar, whenever they gave us a break, I checked on Mace and asked him to come inside with me, but he refused. When the meeting was over for the day, Mace had something to say on the way home about having been left in the car all day. I couldn't believe my ears! After I continually tried to get him to reconsider his decision to stay in the car, I got blamed any way! Note to self.

I had to go back to New York the following day for the second part of the seminar. I didn't want Mace to go with me because I didn't want to hear him complain about being in the car. It's not like he actually had to stay in the car. He was from New York and new it like the back of his hand. It would have been no problem for him to park the car and walk around or drive and visit some old friends. But, apparently, there was a problem.

Mace knew I didn't want to drive by myself and decided that he would go anyway. I really didn't want to have to deal with any chat later on that day, but he was set on going.

152

Finding Mr. Right

He took his time getting ready, knowing I had to be there at a certain time. He knew that I hated being late for anything. He, on the other hand, had the philosophy, "As long as I get there, that is all that matters."

By now, I had also learned that Mace was a little obsessive compulsive. He had to do things in a certain way and order. It bothered me to no end, but I accepted the fact that it was just "him," and I knew that I couldn't change him. I wasn't even going to try.

So, while I was on my way out the back door, Mace was in the bathroom brushing his teeth three times, in a row. He had this thing about brushing his teeth three times whenever he brushed his teeth. As a matter of fact, when he bought things, he had a tendency to buy them in threes as well. He hadn't noticed this until I brought it to his attention. The problem with brushing his teeth three times was that he mostly only did it that one time for the day. So silly me, trying to make sense out of it, asked him about it one day. He simply said, "It's just something I do." Then I commented that it is recommended that we brush our teeth three times a day after meals and not necessarily three times in a row. Oh well, it went in one ear and out the next.

On this particular occasion, I didn't have the time to wait for him to brush his teeth three times because we had to go. It didn't matter with Mace.

Whenever he had somewhere to go, instead of getting ready in advance so he could be on time, he waited until half an hour or so before he was supposed to be there to get ready. This irritated me because it wasn't fair to the other person he was meeting. He didn't care.

As I stood at the back door watching him in the bathroom, I mentioned to him that I was going to the car. As I turned to leave, I heard him swear at me, and I recalled:

"Let no corrupt communication proceed out of your mouth,
but that which is good to the use of edifying, that it may
minister grace unto the heavens." (Ephesians 5:29)

I shook my head as I walked to the car and made up my mind that I didn't want him going with me. There was no way I was going to deal with his silence for the next two and a half hours. It would only ruin my day.

D.Nile Rivers

By the time Mace got to the car, I politely said, "You know, I don't mind going by myself." He ignored me and got in the car. I didn't move. I said, "I would really prefer not to ride in silence with you all the way to New York because you're mad at me right now."

He ordered, "Drive the car."

I told him that I wasn't moving. Mace refused to close his door and refused to leave the car. I saw the potential of things getting ugly, but I kept calm and kept asking him to leave the car so I could go. He didn't care whether I got there or not.

When I couldn't take it any more and after begging and pleading for him to just stay at the house, I walked around to his side of the car and pleaded a little more. I took his hand and playfully said, "Come on Mace, I would rather just go by myself." Of course, I couldn't budge him or persuade him to move. When I tried to tug at his hand as incentive, while at the same time pleading, he did a maneuver with his hand to get me to let go of his hand, which sprained my thumb. It didn't matter to him that he had hurt me. Red Flags!

When I mentioned to him that he hurt my hand, he told me that I grabbed him. He knew that I didn't, but it was his way of justifying his actions.

When I realized that he wasn't going to budge and that time was not waiting for me, I got back in the driver's seat and told him that I was going to drive to the police station for them to help me get him out the car. I asked him to close the door, so I could drive the car, but he kept his right foot outside the car.

Since he wasn't going to budge, I decided to drive with him like that. I tried to turn the car around, but Mace pulled the emergency brake up and caused the car to skid in the middle of my three-point turn, in the middle of the street. I asked him to stop. I tried again and finished the turn only to have him do it again while the car was moving down the road. He didn't care.

I realized that he wasn't going to stop, so I turned the car around and parked it in the driveway at the house. I took out my phone and called his sister. I asked her to talk to him. He took the phone and told her, innocently, that he wasn't doing anything and that it was all me. I yelled so that she could hear me above his lies. I told her to come and get him.

I went back into the house and started taking his things out of the drawers and closet and putting them downstairs on the couch so that

154

Finding Mr. Right

when his sister arrived he would be ready to leave. Well, who told me to do that? When his sister and her boyfriend arrived, Mace was in the bedroom closet refusing to leave. His sister and her boyfriend did what they could to persuade him to leave with them, but he wouldn't listen.

He performed, and I was glad someone else was able to see him in action and witness what I had been dealing with all along.

He told us that the only way he was leaving the house was if we called the police.

I didn't want to call the police because I knew he would act the fool and do something to make them shoot him. Mace had a death wish. He was miserable and hurting inside. He often told me that the only time he would find peace was when he got to heaven. But I knew what the scriptures said.

"Peace I leave with you, my peace I give unto you: not as the world giveth, give I unto you. Let not your heart be troubled, neither let it be afraid." (John 14:27)

It didn't matter what I quoted from the Bible; I was always accused of not knowing what I was talking about. Even when I knew God had given me understanding of His Word, Mace would accuse me of using the Scriptures out of context. I had heard this so many times from him that I got to the point where I second guessed myself and my understanding of the Bible.

I explained to his sister what happened and told her that I didn't want him in the house any more. She begged him to listen to her and to think of all I had already done for him and how much I loved him. It didn't matter what she said. She eventually got him to come out of the closet and got him to go downstairs. I didn't follow them. I laid on the bed exhausted. I didn't want to go through this anymore.

After a while, I heard a door shut and went downstairs to see if they had finally gotten him to leave. By now, they had been there approximately three hours trying to coerce him to leave. I felt relieved, thinking that they had left, but when I got downstairs, Mace was still in the house and so were his things. I ran outside to stop his sister from leaving, but she drove away. I couldn't believe it. I was in trouble now. I had gotten his family involved.

Strangely enough, he didn't do anything to me. I reluctantly put his things back in the drawers and the closets because he wouldn't do

D.Nile Rivers

it. He was angry with me and he didn't mind showing it. He told me that he wasn't leaving, and the only way it would happen was if I called the police. He knew I wouldn't do it.

As a result of my actions, I was on punishment again. He walked about the house ignoring me, knowing very well that it bothered me more than anything else. I just prayed.

Every morning I woke up and asked God to give me love for him and every day I was polite and continued to do and be the wife that I had committed to being. But it wasn't easy. He purposely made it difficult.

The incidents continued. In between, there were good times. I recall Mace saying to me one day, "I can be the best husband you ever had, and I can be the worst husband you ever had." He knew exactly what he was doing.

Little by little, Mace broke me down. I didn't realize it, but he had set out to do this from the start.

"The thief cometh not, but for to steal, and to kill, and to destroy: I am come that they might have life, and that they might have it more abundantly." (John 10:10)

In his mind, he was like Jeremiah and often told me to read the first chapter of the book of Jeremiah. He said that he was sent to root out, to pull down, and to build back up. Whenever he said this, I checked my recollection of the scriptures, and I just couldn't agree with him. I just held on to the fact that God wouldn't bring me to where I was to have someone come into my life to break me down and totally destroy me. It was contrary to what I felt and what I believed, but I stayed in the mess I was in.

Aside from the physical abuse, he worked on me verbally, mentally, and emotionally. But he did it in such a way that I didn't realize it. He was cunning, but he didn't hide what he did. He made no excuses for his behavior. He simply stated that he was the way he was, and that that wasn't going to change.

I got to a point where I could sense his moods. One minute he would be happy, and without warning he would get very angry. I understood that there was a war going on inside of him, and all I did was pray and ask God to deliver him, except he didn't want to be delivered. He told me that he kept his anger close because it reminded

156

Finding Mr. Right

him of where he'd been and where he didn't want to go back to. He said that it kept him pushing forward. I checked my recollection of the scriptures again on anger.

"But now ye also put off all these; anger, wrath, malice, blasphemy, filthy communication out of your mouth." (Colossians 3:8)

One time he even said to me, "Vengeance is mine." I couldn't believe it because I know the scripture says, "...Vengeance is mine: I will repay, saith the Lord." (Romans 12:19)

I listened to the things he said, and I checked the Bible. I knew that the two didn't match up, yet there were times when I felt God was speaking through him. Based on these times, I just knew that God would prevail. It's not that God couldn't prevail; it was that Mace didn't want Him to.

Based on Mace's moods and all that I was going through, I went for counseling. He wouldn't go, so I went and talked about what I was going through. From what I told the counselor, she mentioned that Mace might be bi-polar. I didn't know anything about it, but I looked it up and based on the symptoms I would agree that he was, but in all reality, I just felt that he had such a battle going on inside of him that the enemy had a tendency to win over his desire to serve God.

Regardless, I was in the mist of a storm, and it was only getting worse. To avoid dealing with Mace when his mood went south, I got into the habit of trying to be around people when it happened, or if we were in the car, I would exit the car and wait for him to cool off. If I was at my wits end, I would simply ask him to leave, and he would disappear for a few months always threatening never to enter my house again. When he did come back, he would say that God told him to "Dwell with me with understanding." I wasn't buying that anymore. I took him back because I kept trying to stand by the commitment I made.

When Mace finally broke me down, when I no longer bounced back and was cheerful after an episode of dealing with him, when I looked and felt beaten, he simply said, "See, told you no one could be as happy as you all the time."

I couldn't believe my ears, but I couldn't feel sorry for myself either because I hadn't listened.

157

D.Nile Rivers

He told me one day that he felt everything that I did for him had an ulterior motive. I couldn't believe it. I threw up my hands and exclaimed that there was nothing else I could do to show him that I loved him and was sincere about it.

I wanted to give in and give up. I wanted to go back to my old self before I got saved and act the fool. I wanted to ignore him like he ignored me, but I woke up the next day, and God had placed love in my heart for him, yet again, and I remembered the verse:

"And let us not be weary in well doing: for in due season we
shall reap, if we faint not." (Galatians 6:9)

So I prayed and asked God for the strength to keep going. And I did. I believed that God knew my heart, and He knew that I was trying to do right as a wife and as a Christian.

Almost a year after we were married, it was revealed to me that what I was actually dealing with were the consequences of my disobedience in marrying him. I accepted this revelation and I was able to repent.

Once I realized this, I shared this with Mace, but he didn't want to hear it. So I repented and asked forgiveness from Pastor as well as my mentor. They told me that they still loved me and were praying for me the entire time. I knew they had to be because there was no way that my prayers were enough for the demons I was dealing with.

They prayed for me and with me from time to time, but because I was still back and forth in the midst of the marital storm, I continued to deal with and endured the consequences of my actions.

I went to them for guidance regarding a divorce, but no one wanted to say the actual words whether I should or not. I really didn't blame them because I had made the decision to marry Mace on my own, despite their warnings not to. I figured that I had gotten myself into this mess; I would get myself out.

I just didn't want to make any more decisions without permission. So, I kept praying and seeking God for His will, but I couldn't hear from God like I used to. I didn't trust any of the voices I heard, because I had listened to the wrong one to begin with and look where it got me. I was so afraid to make the wrong decision because I just knew I couldn't deal with any more consequences. I just didn't have the strength any more.

158

Chapter Twenty-Five

The Beginning of the End

I got to a place in my life and my relationship with Mace where I needed to make a decision. Unfortunately, I didn't know what to do and I was afraid of doing the wrong thing in the sight of God. I was extremely fearful of having to deal with consequences.

Things between us hadn't gotten any better and two years had already gone by. It had been a very painful and devastating two years. I knew that it was only because of the Grace of God that I was still breathing.

When I looked back on where I started, to where I ended up, I knew it had nothing to do with God, but was a result of my own doing. I felt like a fool, and ashamed. I didn't have a problem admitting that I had made a mistake to anyone who asked. Sure, I had bragged about knowing that Mace was the *One* when all along he wasn't. I was left in a state where I didn't trust myself to make *any* decisions. It didn't matter what it was.

The enemy had fooled me into accepting his gift, which turned out to be nothing more than an attempt to defeat me and kill me. It almost seemed like it would work, but God had other plans for my life. He allowed me to endure my mess until I came to the realization that I had turned my back on Him, for a man. I lost my intimacy with Him because I wasn't at a point in my life where I knew how to keep God first and be in a relationship at the same time. Once again, I had let God down and I was ashamed. I was broken, beaten, and weak, but I wasn't ready to give up yet. I wasn't about to let the enemy win.

My experience with Mace had me in such a state that I literally had to be purified, purged, restored, redeemed, and replenished.

D.Nile Rivers

When I looked back on where I was when I met Mace, to where I ended up, it saddened me, because I wasn't the person I used to be and it was nobody's fault but my own.

Mace took off again. The funny thing is, when he left, we were on speaking terms. He was going away for business reasons, so he said, and would be back within a couple weeks. Once he left, I really didn't want him to come back, at least not to me.

It took my daughter calling 911, and the police threatening to arrest me, for me to come to my senses! It should never have gotten to that point.

It wasn't anything out of the ordinary. He had threatened to kill me yet again. I had heard it before, and each time I believed him, but I wasn't afraid. The only difference this time was the fact that Morgan was in the house during the altercation. I got her involved when I yelled upstairs from the basement and asked her to call 911. She had no idea why she was calling. She hadn't heard any screaming or anything. She might have heard things being thrown around if she was paying attention, but I don't think she was.

The thing that did it for me was the fact that in the midst of my beating, Mace carefully took my glasses off my face, placed them on my compact disk rack, and punched me in my eye like I was a man. To this day, I still think of that specific thing, even more than the fact that I could barely speak from the pressure he had put on my throat. Never mind the fact that I had a problem swallowing and had to go to a throat specialist a few days later. Just the thought of him, maliciously planning the steps to hit me the way he did, left more of an impact on me.

What started it this time? Once again, I tried to deal with his smug indifference, and neglect the best way I could and for as long as I could. As usual, he was in the office in the basement wasting time like he had done for the past two years, waiting on God to do what God was waiting on him to do. He just didn't get it. In his mind, everybody else was wrong and only he was right. Sounds like the old me.

After much deliberation, I went down to the office to try to reason with him and express to him how I felt. I was tired of leaving the house and spending days at my girlfriend's house simply to keep my sanity while he continued on in the basement like no one else existed.

I interrupted his writing. I had shown him how to use Word Perfect on the computer and he had taken on the responsibility of typing his

160

Finding Mr. Right

own poems, which he did all day and every day. It took him eight hours to type two poems. He was amazingly slow.

I asked him if I could talk to him, and he slowly stopped what he was doing to listen. When I was finished, he had a smirk on his face which irritated me, but I kept my cool. As he started to speak, he went into his thug mode and proceeded to speak to me like I was some man in the street. I stopped him and asked, "Is your attitude towards me necessary right now?"

He said, "This is who I am."

By the time the conversation was done, he said that he had nothing further to say and dismissed me. He knew how much I hated to be dismissed, especially when I was making the effort to try to speak to him; something we had agreed to do. I felt stupid for having made the effort. I felt stupid for constantly being rejected and dismissed after all I had gone through with him; all the times I had taken him back and forgiven him.

I tried to walk away, but instead, I went back into the office and slammed my hand down on the computer keyboard to get his attention. Who told me to do that? He sat back in the chair and smiled. He knew exactly what he had done. He knew exactly how to push my buttons, and he liked it. When that didn't work, I opened a file drawer where I kept my floppy disks and removed one that I had been saving his poems on that I had typed for him. He didn't like this too much. So, in the blink of an eye, he grabbed my wrist and pushed me backwards. He held me at an angle (in a corner) between the desk and shelf that had my two computer printers. The only thing holding me up was him not letting me go. He took the disk out of my hand, and instead of it ending with him getting his disk, he commenced to punishing me. He told me that he was going to kill me and I believed him. Within minutes, he started to cry and walked away. I knew he didn't intentionally want to hurt me, but I also knew that it wouldn't prevent him from killing me one day. I took his moment of weakness as my opportunity to leave.

I went upstairs, packed an overnight bag with clothes for Morgan and myself. By the time I was finished packing and heading to the car, the police arrived.

Unfortunately, being called to my house for domestic altercation had become the norm over the past two years. Fortunately for me, the officers who responded were officers I was familiar with and were

D.Nile Rivers

officers who knew me enough to know that it wasn't the norm for me to attack people, let alone a man almost twice my size.

Two of the officers went into the house to speak to Mace, while one of the officers, Kurt, a friend of mine, stayed outside to hear my side of the story. First of all, he couldn't believe I had let Mace back into my life and house after all I'd been through previously.

He said, "You know better."

I said, "I know."

All I could do was shake my head and hold my throat as I tried to speak. But before I could even finish speaking, I began to cry. I didn't want him to see me crying, so I turned my back to him and just shook my head. I wasn't used to any one seeing me cry. I always displayed a tough guy attitude, and I wanted to keep it that way, but I was truly broken.

After a while, the two officers exited the house and told me that Mace had told them pretty much what I had already told them about the situation. Regardless, because he had scratches on him, it was their duty to arrest us both. I explained to them that he got scratched after I tried to defend myself, but it didn't matter. I had forgotten that the law stated that if both parties showed signs of abuse that it was a mandatory arrest for both parties. I wasn't a police officer any more, so I had forgotten.

I thought about my daughter who was sitting in my car at the time, and I thought about how he got the scratches. I explained to them that after he wouldn't stop hitting me, I fought back by scratching him. It didn't matter, but there was no way I was going to jail for him putting his hands on me.

They asked, "What do you want us to do?"

I said, "I don't want him to go to jail, and I don't want to go to jail."

I told them that I was leaving anyway, and that I would file for a restraining order (my second one) the next day.

Kurt looked at me and said, "You better file for a restraining order tomorrow!"

I promised that I would and left.

I just knew that I would have black and blue marks all over my body and a black eye the following day, but when I looked in the mirror, there was no black eye. All I had as evidence was a busted lip. I pressed on my eye and it hurt around the socket area, but there was no

Finding Mr. Right

bruising. I didn't understand it. I knew I hadn't made up the part where he punched me in my eye! Any other month I had been hit, there was evidence of black and blue marks and the aches to prove it. I later thought that, in God keeping me from dying that night, he also allowed me to come out unscathed. To God be ALL the glory!

The following day I went to the courthouse and filed for a restraining order. I was embarrassed, because I had already filed for one the previous year and had dismissed it after the initial ten days had passed. Here I was again, appearing before the judge, for the same thing and with the same person.

It wasn't so much that I was embarrassed, but the fact that I was trained as a domestic violence investigator and I knew better. I knew that once he hit me that he would continue to do it, but I just believed that he would be delivered. Unfortunately, it wasn't something he thought warranted deliverance.

The judge granted the temporary restraining order until he could be served and had the opportunity to appear before the judge to tell his side of the story.

Well, by Monday (the incident happened on a Friday), I filed for a divorce. I spent the weekend praying and asking God to tell me what to do. I, not God, concluded that God didn't want me to be in the midst of the mess I was in. I decided that this wasn't God's will for my life because there was no way He would have wanted me to end up where I was, broken by this man and not by God Himself.

By the time Friday, August 4, 2005 rolled around, and we had to appear before the judge, I had already talked myself out of what I had done. I, or the enemy, convinced me that I had acted based on emotions and not because God had spoken to me. So, by the time we got before the judge, instead of keeping the restraining order against Mace, I told the judge that we had agreed to stay away from each other. We did. We had spoken on the phone and agreed that we needed some time apart. I also told the judge to cancel the request for the divorce. I just didn't know if I was doing the right thing. I kept thinking about what the Bible said about divorce, and knew that it wasn't something pleasing to God. I didn't cancel it because I wanted to stay with him because I didn't. There was nothing in my mind, at this point, telling me that I should be with him. There was nothing in my heart left to give him either.

We left the courthouse and went to the house to get some of his

163

belongings. I told him that I would take him to the bus station, but I agreed to take him to get something to eat first.

On the way, I told him that I didn't cancel the divorce because I wanted to be with him. I also told him that I couldn't think of being with him either. He mentioned something about when he got back and about us, but I immediately told him that I wasn't thinking about that. I told him that I didn't see us living under the same roof any time soon. He agreed, and said that we would talk about it.

When I dropped him off at the bus station, he kissed me as if things were great between us. I let him. There was nothing in my mind that resembled anything close to us being great. I simply let him believe that it was, long enough to send him on his way.

Once he was gone, I went on with my life. He, on the other hand, kept calling me to talk. I eventually told him that I needed some time to myself. He misunderstood and thought I meant for that day, when, in reality, I needed a week, or more. When I refused to return his calls, he got angry. I didn't care. I told him that I didn't have anything to say to him, and I didn't know when I would.

During his absence, I did a lot of soul searching, praying, and fasting. What amazed me the most was my ability to completely forget that he even existed. He was out of sight and definitely out of mind. It wasn't until I was asked, "How is your husband?" that I remembered that I was still married. There was nothing in my heart for him, and I had closed off my thoughts regarding him at this point. The only proof of his existence was his things on the front porch, which he refused to pick up. I packed up all his belongings and placed them in boxes. I inventoried each box and taped the list on the outside so he would know what each box contained.

I decided to contact his aunt about getting rid of any remaining existence of him in the house. She wasn't speaking to me at this point. She had listened to everything he had told her regarding me, that I attacked him and that I was crazy. Never mind the fact that I had tried to explain to her a year before about what I had been going through. She told me that she had known him all his life, and she couldn't believe that the person I was referring to was her nephew. It hurt to know that she thought I would make up such a story, but I let it go.

I was afraid to call her. Mace had threatened me in the past and had hit me for getting his family involved in anything I was going through. But I prayed and picked up the phone. When she answered,

Finding Mr. Right

she was polite, and I was relieved that she was willing to speak to me. I explained to her that Mace refused to pick up his things, and, as a result, I was putting his things in storage and sending her the key so that she could pass it on to him. I explained to her that if I was a vindictive person that I would have thrown his things away, but I didn't want to do that. I told her that I had rented the storage for a month in order to give him enough time to get his things. She thought about it and expressed to me that she thought it was reasonable and mentioned that she would talk to him about it.

I also told her what had transpired and why we weren't together. She had no idea! She couldn't believe that I had a restraining order against him or anything else that had happened. I agreed to send her the reports, the restraining orders and any other information or paperwork I could find to verify my story. I did just that.

When she received all that I had sent her, she couldn't believe it. She had to see it to believe it. She finally understood what I had been through and understood why I couldn't do it any more. She told me that she would confront him about the restraining orders, and I begged her to pray first. I reminded her that my life depended on what she said to him. She still had problems believing that he was dangerous, but I didn't want to have to die for her to believe it.

Five months after he left, I called him and left a message asking him what he was planning on doing about dissolving this farce of a marriage. He didn't return the call. I tried once more before I decided to call his aunt to ask her to relay the message.

She said, "He doesn't want to talk to you."

That was fine with me, but I told her, "Well, I don't want to talk to him either, but things need to be discussed regarding a divorce."

She told me that she would talk to him. It didn't matter to me if he wanted to speak to me. I needed to speak to him. He called later on that night.

I asked, "What are your plans regarding this joke of a marriage we are in?"

He said, "It's not at the top of my list of things to do right now."

I reminded him that I had paid for the divorce the last time, before I cancelled it, and I didn't have the money to file again.

He said, "I don't have the money, either."

"Well are you planning on getting the money?" I asked.

"I am not thinking about that right now." He said.

165

D.Nile Rivers

"Well, when do you think you might have the money?" I asked.

"I don't know." He said.

That was pretty much the way the conversation went. But before I hung up, I said, "When you think you have the money or you find the time, could you let me know?"

That was in December 2005. By the time January 2006 rolled around, I was all set to bring in the New Year without any excess baggage. I didn't want anything left of Mace in my life, not even his last name to associate me with him, so I filed for a divorce. I contacted his aunt and told her, and she told me to take care of myself.

Chapter Twenty-Six

Finding Mr. Right

It was time to rebuild and pick up the pieces of my life. I literally felt like a jigsaw puzzle scattered here and there. I felt like I had to reach in corners and under debris to find pieces of myself that were no longer a part of my being. And as I found them, I placed them back where they belonged, but they didn't fit snuggly like they used to. Instead, they were a little warped and frayed, squished and smashed, so that the pieces didn't interlock tightly. I was a mess, and I knew it. I felt it, and I just knew it showed. I couldn't pretend, never could.

I smiled, but it never reached my eyes; it didn't come from my heart. I laughed but it echoed sadness. My spirit was broken, but not by God. I literally felt like a walking zombie. I wanted to run away and disappear, but I couldn't because of Morgan. If it weren't for Morgan, disappearing wouldn't be a problem. But I couldn't do that to her, and I knew that I couldn't run away from myself.

I prayed. I cried out to God to help me, because I just couldn't get up from my spiritual doom. Depression threatened to take me over, but I continued to pray.

The devil wasn't letting up. He kept trying to keep me down and bury me with feelings of shame and despair. He kept reminding me of how I had let God down because I hadn't listened.

I wanted to punish myself for letting God down. I couldn't believe I had been so stupid! How did I get here? Why was I here? I got here because I didn't listen. But I was still here, breathing because God was not through with me yet.

God had kept me from the hands of the enemy who wanted nothing more than to kill and destroy me.

D.Nile Rivers

Through it all, I continued to go to church, and I continued to pray. I had never prayed so much in all my life! But even though I prayed and went to church, even though I would be strengthened and renewed, it didn't last. It didn't last because I still didn't get it.

Every time I got strengthened and renewed, I felt I could deal with the situation. I felt that I was supposed to deal with the situation. I was wrong.

I didn't understand what it meant when my mentor told me not to have sex. He never said how long; he just said not to. But I was married to this man and the Bible said:

"Defraud ye not one the other, except it be with consent for a time, that ye may give yourselves to fasting and prayer; and come together again, that Satan tempt you not for your incontinency." (1 Corinthians 7:5)

I thought about it and I didn't have a problem "not" having sex because I was at a point in my life where it wasn't about that any more. Not to mention the fact that Mace tried to use sex as a punishment by not having sex until he wanted to. Once I realized that he thought he could use this against me, I made up in my mind that I wouldn't let it bother me.

Even so, I was available, as his wife, to please him. I didn't realize, that in having sex with him, I was uniting my spirit with whatever spirits were associated with him. I wasn't thinking about the whole act of sex. I couldn't call it "making love" because that was something he and I didn't do. He might have thought we were, but it wasn't. The majority of the time I just felt like he had something to prove, and the only thing it proved to me was that it wasn't about me.

I knew what the scripture said, "Wherefore they are no more twain, but one flesh..." (Matthew 19:6)

I had forgotten the meaning of, "one" flesh. Regardless of whether or not we weren't making love, we were still coming together and that made us one. I repeatedly performed the act of becoming "one" with the enemy! Oh My God! I didn't think of it that way. I didn't think; period.

Every time I was intimate with this man, I weighed myself down with whatever was in him, and it took its toll on me. But God, He saw Everything and kept me until I was able to see what it was I couldn't

Finding Mr. Right

see.

He kept me alive when I should have been dead. He gave me the strength to keep pushing when the enemy wanted me to lay down and die. He kept my mind when the enemy tried to consume me with thoughts of despair.

When I finally got the revelation of where God had brought me from, all I could do was cry and give God praise. When He literally showed me (like on a screen) how I was buried, six feet under, based on all I had been through, all I could do was give Him thanks. He showed me my life and how the enemy tried to kill me, how the enemy tried to destroy what God had built, and I cried because I was ashamed.

Prior to Mace, I was so on fire for God. I never thought the enemy had a shot at breaking me down, but it happened. Because God was in control, the enemy couldn't succeed. Like Job, the devil didn't have permission to kill me. Yes, I had gotten myself into the mess I was in, and God allowed me to go through it, but He gave me the strength to endure it. The enemy had his limits.

God brought me back from the deep, and as He did so, I was able to shed some pain and some hurt; some resentment and some shame. I wanted it to happen all at once, but God knew what I was able to handle. I wanted to get back to where I was with God, but God knew it would take a process. It took a process to get me to where I was, beaten and broken, so why did I think getting back to where I needed to be would happen over night?

I had to go through some things. Certain things had to be revealed to me. I needed to understand why I kept falling into the same trap. Why? I needed answers because I didn't want to ever be where I was again. So, I prayed and sought God for the answers. I needed help, and I needed it now!

I took time out to analyze my ways, my needs, my wants, my heart, my issues. As I sought God, He began to restore me, to show me His love, to give me understanding of myself. He revealed things about me that I needed to be delivered from.

In this particular chapter of my life, I came to understand that I was in a vulnerable position. The enemy knew it and took advantage of it. Why shouldn't he have? It's his job to try to destroy me! He was trying to destroy what God had done in my life thus far, trying to keep me from going further in Christ.

I realized that I had never dealt with Manny's passing. I kept going on with life as usual, accepting the fact that he was gone, and that I would always miss him. The truth was, I didn't know how to grieve. I was afraid to grieve because I wasn't sure I could control it and I just had to be in control at all times! Not a good way to be.

What I have learned now is that my issues didn't start or end with Manny. My issues started way back when I was a child. Something was missing.

I have learned that we all have basic needs, whether physical, emotional, or spiritual. This is nothing new. When these needs are unmet, it creates a void within us that in turn causes us to search for fulfillment of these needs. Many times, what we meet the needs with, does more harm than good.

Until we understand our needs and ourselves first, we will continually find ourselves in a cycle of trying to find ways to meet these needs. It's like trying to fix a leak without knowing what is causing the leak. If you don't know the root of the problem or the source of the leak, you will never be able to fix the problem. Anything you do will always be a temporary solution to a much bigger problem that you haven't taken the time to understand.

For me, I kept trying to fix the problem, but I had no idea what the root of the problem was. As far back as I could remember, I was always looking for something. To think of the many times I thought I had found what I was looking for in someone, only to be disappointed because it just wasn't quite it; even in the most compatible of people. I came to the understanding that I could never find everything I needed in a man because if I did I wouldn't need God. It made sense to me. God wouldn't create me in such a way that I wouldn't need him. What would be the point?

I came to understand that God *has* to remain first and foremost in my life. I know that I've been told many times that I am supposed to keep God first, and I've tried. But every time I let someone in, I allowed myself to get consumed with how I felt for them and my desire to be with them, which meant my thoughts were always on them and not on God. If my thoughts aren't on God, that gives the enemy a way in. I knew this, but I thought I could balance the two. I couldn't. I would love one and disregard the other. The Bible does say that we can't have two masters!

Finding Mr. Right

"No man can serve two masters: for either he will hate the one, and love the other; or else he will hold to the one, and despise the other. Ye cannot serve God and mammon." (Matthew 6:24)

I knew that the Bible said to seek things that are above and the kingdom of God. I understood that, but now I understand that there is also a part of me yearning and seeking a love that I thought I could find in a man, not realizing that I could only find it in God. I kept looking for a "Mr. Right," meaning he would be perfect in every way, thinking that what I needed in a man would satisfy my needs when, in reality, no man could do or give me what I needed. Finally!

God revealed to me, through His Holy Spirit, that if He made it so that we were able to get everything we needed in our mates, then we wouldn't need Him. He said, "All you need is Me." That hit me like one of Mace's punches, smack dab in the head.

With that, I gained a better understanding of who I was in that moment. When I looked back over my life and my relationships, I was able to see how my unrealistic expectations and misguided information from society had influenced my perception of what I needed.

I wanted somebody to understand me, to show me affection, and pay me some attention. I wanted somebody to communicate with and someone to hear me. I wanted someone to make me feel whole. No man or woman has the ability to do that for anyone; they are not God! Better to learn it later than never.

Based on this realization, I had to step back and check myself. I was wrong in my expectations of the men in my life. I expected them to be to me what only God could be: EVERYTHING. Sure, God created man and woman to be together, "And the Lord God said, It is not good that the man should be alone; I will make him an help meet for him" (Genesis 2:18); but man has limitations; whereas, God has none. Man is not perfect and is prone to err. God is omnipotent. Man will disappoint you and let you down. God will never leave you nor forsake you. God is faithful; He is gracious and merciful. He is God!

Well, I knew all this because I have read it, and I have heard it, but I had to talk to God about it. I said, "God, you created me so you know my needs. You know exactly how I am. You know that I crave the touch of a man, his hugs, his kisses, and his presence. If you created me, then you know I have these needs. If you don't want me to keep trying to fulfill these needs with worldly means, then I am going to

D.Nile Rivers

need your help on this one."

I said, "I don't want to keep going from man to man, trying to fill this void, especially since I have come to realize that they can't fill it anyway. So, if they can't fill it, and only you can fill it, God, then can you just help a sister out? I could really use some help!"

I had to go way back to figure out some things. What exactly did I get from these needs that I wanted a man to fill? What exactly was it that I was looking for them to do? When they held me, what did I get from it? It felt safe and comfortable. When they kissed me, what did I get from it? I got excited and wanted to have sex. When I had sex with them, what did I get from it? Disappointment most of the time, because, even though it gave me physical pleasure or relieved some frustration, once it was over, the void was still there. Wow! I just got that. So, if I was doing all this to fill a void, but the void still remained unfilled at the end of the act, what exactly was I looking for them to do for me?

Men are not the answer. Sure, they serve a purpose, whether it's for companionship, friendship, affection, attention, etc., but they are not the answer.

When I stopped and thought about the times I had been happy in a relationship, they were always when I kept God first. I always felt happy when I was able to communicate with God and have Him speak to me and reveal things to me. Whenever someone said to me, "Wow, marriage agrees with you," I would always smile and tell them, "No, it's God." It always went over their heads. They couldn't possibly understand unless they had a relationship with God.

I have come to understand that a man couldn't make me happy. Besides, happiness is temporary, but the joy God gives is everlasting. A man might make me feel good at times, but being in a relationship with a man doesn't guarantee me happiness. God, on the other hand, has a whole lot of guarantees, and if I have to choose between man and God, I choose God because He has proven to me to be EVERYTHING I need.

Epilogue

When I told women about this book, they immediately got excited. Their desire to find "Mr. Right" was just as prevalent as mine. Like me, many of them have been through some detours, speed bumps, pot holes, construction sites, etc., on their journey, and as a result, they are weary and want to rest. They just want the security and assurance of being able to rest with that special someone in their life. Is that too much to ask?

Once I realized that I was looking for something that I could never find in a man, when I realized that what I really needed was to be able to accept the kind of love only God could give me, my journey took on whole new meaning.

I was under the impression that I *had t*o find what I needed in a man in order to live happily ever after. I wanted the fairytale romance and the *Lifetime for Women* happy ending that I saw on television. Don't believe everything you see on television.

Even now when I see a romance movie and I wish I could have a happy ending like they portray. Society and the media can really mess you up. It can entice you and make you seek after the *unrealistic* dream. I won't say the *impossible* dream because I know that with God, all things are possible.

First, I had to identify that I had a need. Then I had to find out how to fill the need. I kept trying to fill my need, but because I didn't understand what the need was, I kept using the wrong means to fill it. Like I mentioned in the book, you have to get to the root of the problem.

I knew that the only way I could understand what I needed was to seek God for help. I had tried on my own and I was weary of ending up in the same place. I needed something different to happen. I was desperate.

D.Nile Rivers

I went on a forty-day fast. I needed to hear from God and I knew that I couldn't hear Him where I was. I needed to consecrate myself to Him. Desperate times require desperate measures.

I realized that my need was love and affection. I wanted to feel loved and my way of doing that was by getting involved with men. Unfortunately, I never ended up with what I wanted.

When I look back over my life, I can truly say that I never got what I wanted. If I had, I would still be with at least one of them right now. I truly believed that they loved me, but it wasn't the kind of love I needed. I had a problem.

I went to God for answers. I came to understand that the kind of love I needed, I could only get from God. I had to analyze what it was I really needed. I looked back over my relationships and I analyzed what each man did for me. I realized that even with what they offered as love, it wasn't quite right. Then I thought about God. I checked the scriptures and every where I turned I read of how much God loved me. Then I thought of my life and how He kept me from death; how He cancelled the orders for my son to go to war; how He provided food to eat when I didn't know where the money was coming from; how He kept my house from going to foreclosure; how He sent His son, Jesus Christ, to die in my place; how He strengthened me and kept me when I wanted to give up.

When I think of all God has done for me, I know that He loves me in ways that no one else could. When I think of all the dirt I've done and the people I've hurt…and still He forgave me, it amazes me.

I think of the men in my past and I know that they couldn't love me like God does. They didn't have the ability to love me past my hurt, my pain, and my faults. But I expected them to. That was my fault. I got caught up in the fantasy of TV land and fairy tales. I expected them to be, what I had imagined.

But I still wanted to be hugged, touched, kissed, etc. I understood that I needed to look to God to meet my unmet needs of affection, but I couldn't touch Him, see Him, or hold Him. I still needed and wanted that. God had a plan for that as well.

I was determined to have my unmet needs met. I was determined to overcome and/or be delivered from my never ending cycle of failed relationships. I was determined *to do something I had never done in order to get something I had never had*. It wasn't a wish or a want; it was a must.

Finding Mr. Right

I had a talk with God. I reminded Him that I still wanted the hands on part of my needs met, but He had a plan. He let me know that once I was able to look to Him for everything and not just some things; once I was able to give Him my heart totally, which would allow me to keep Him first when I was involved in a relationship, then He would take care of the physical. God was waiting on me!

He knew that I wasn't in a place where I could keep Him first. He saw me getting involved, thinking I could handle it and trying the best I could, but He knew that it wouldn't work. He also knew that I would have to learn the hard way. He needed me to get to the place where I had had enough, before I would allow Him to do what He had to do in my life. When I got to that place, He knew that I was ready to listen.

God began to show me His love by the things He did for me. Every time He forgave me for messing up; every time He blessed me in my time of need, He showed me His love. He just kept giving and doing, and all I could do was smile and tell Him, "Thank you." The more He did, the closer I got to Him. The closer I got to Him, the fuller the void got. The more I was able to grasp God's love for me, the less I felt the need for the physical. I was so focused on God's love that there wasn't room for anything else. That doesn't mean I didn't want the physical, it just meant that my obsession with the physical wasn't trying to overtake me any more. My needs were more balanced.

When our needs are out of balance, we become messed up; whether it is our physical, spiritual, or emotional needs. If only one or two needs are being met, then there's a problem because all three needs aren't balanced. We have to get to a place where we are balanced, and we can only get there with God's help.

Now that my focus wasn't so much on the physical and God was fulfilling my needs for affection, I was able to experience the love I was looking for and then some. I thought I understood love, but I didn't. My perception of love wasn't even close to what I found in God. It's not temporary, it's not conditional, it's not greedy, selfish, arrogant, envious, or full of anger.

"Love is patient and kind. Love is not jealous or boastful or proud or rude. Love does not demand its own way. Love is not irritable, and it keeps no record of when it has been wronged. It is never glad about injustice but rejoices

D.Nile Rivers

whenever the truth wins out. Love never gives up, never loses faith, is always hopeful, and endures through every circumstance." (1 Corinthians 13:4-7)

Whenever a man told me that he loved me and did things contrary to what love meant, I didn't believe him. I always told him, "Prove it." I needed to be shown love because I had heard it too many times and it just wasn't adding up.

I always thought that if a man loved me, he would take the time to know me and learn what it was I needed. Once again, I expected him to be God and he wasn't.

God knew exactly what I needed because He created me. But because I didn't trust Him enough and wanted to do things my own way, He decided to give me enough rope…knowing He wouldn't let me hang myself.

I thank God for my journey and all the things that I have learned along the way. Even though the experiences weren't always pleasant, I have learned from them. Some of them I had to experience a few times because I didn't quite get it the first time.

Sometimes we get caught up in cycles and it takes years before we actually realize that we are actually in a cycle. Some realize it sooner than others; they learn the lesson and keep on moving. Others are not so fortunate. Like me, they learn the hard way.

Once you realize you're in a cycle, it's up to you to get out. If you are content being in the cycle, there is no desire or motivation to get out. If you think that the other person is going to do it for you, then you've got a problem.

If you are looking for "Mr. Right," check with God first. He knows exactly what you need, especially if you don't. Even if you think you know, still check with God first. He is the only one you should be looking for.

I've been married three times and each one was riddled with issues. I knew that marriages had issues, but I kept butting up against the same issues. I kept choosing the wrong men. The Bible says, "Whoso findeth a wife findeth a good thing, and obtaineth favour of the Lord" (Proverbs 18:22). It doesn't say, "She who findeth a husband findeth a good thing." I was trying to do a rewrite. I was looking for a husband when I should have been trying to get right with God. I kept seeking men and choosing them, when it wasn't my place to do so.

176

Finding Mr. Right

When I saw something I wanted, I went for it. I never thought I had to wait on a man and I didn't. But I didn't wait on God either. Be careful what you look for; you just might get it.

If you are reading this, and you don't have a relationship with God, you might be a little perplexed. You might wonder 'how' it could be possible to find everything you need in a God you can't see, hold, or feel. It is possible.

God created you and He knows exactly what you need. He knows everything about you. Since He created you and knows you better than anyone else, it only makes sense to turn to Him for the answers you seek.

God loves you so much that He sent His son, Jesus Christ, to die so that you can have hope and everlasting life (John 3:16). He made a way in advance, knowing that you would be exactly where you are today. But there is hope; all you have to do is believe.

The Bible says, "For whosoever shall call upon the name of the Lord shall be saved." All you have to do is believe and receive Jesus Christ as your Savior. Confess with your mouth and believing in your heart that God raised Him from the dead and you will be saved. "For it is by believing in your heart that you are made right with God, and it is by confessing with your mouth that you are saved." (Romans 10:9-10 & 13)

If you are looking and not finding what it is you are looking for, why not give God a try? All you have to lose is your life.

"He that findeth his life shall lose it: and he that loseth his life for my sake shall find it." (Matthew 10:39)

My prayer: Father God in Heaven, thank You for Your love and Your mercy towards us. Thank You for the person who may be reading this prayer right now. Father, I pray that he or she be willing to seek You for change from this day forward. May you strengthen him or her on the journey to living for You, in Jesus name, I pray. Amen.